PSYCHOLOGICAL DISORDERS AND YOUR PERSONALITY

YOU ARE WHO YOU ARE

Aaron McKennith

CONTENT

INTRODUCTION

The nature of certain behaviors that are considered destructive can vary from person to person. However, most experts agree that psychological disorders threaten (or damage) the physical integrity, property, space, or daily functioning of a person. In this way, psychological disorders usually affect the rights of others, but you can control it yourself. Candidates most likely to be classified as destructive are behaviors classified as aggressive, especially when the level of aggression is so high that they can be considered verbal or physical violence. Physical aggression can include attacking or destroying others, but it can also be self-directed and include self-incitement or attempted suicide. Verbal aggression is usually directed at others and usually involves screaming, threats, naming and various forms of verbal intimidation. In short, the aggressive behavior described above is the type of behavior that is considered psychological according to the operational definitions defined in this book.

However, psychological behavior may not always be associated with aggression. For example, they can impede the ability of others to benefit from education (e.g. when a student acts or the teacher's ability to teach in the classroom) to focus on work (for example when a coworker gives impulses, moves too well, feels comfortable in the environment You (e.g. when others around you talk excessively or not) and support appropriate social interactions (e.g. when other people talk or social interactions) interruptions)).

Lack of adequate impulse control is often the cause of psychological disorders. When you get a response - for example, when you are angry, or when you move, say, or do something - most people can control these reactions and are usually harmless unless the stimulus is insignificant. Stress exceeds normal self-control (e.g. if a partner determines that another partner is having an affair). However, some people have little control over daily triggers and respond to many of their impulses with words and behavior, apparently unable to control their internal needs. Therefore, this book conceptualizes psychological disorders, such as those caused by internal impulses, that most people can suppress in certain situations, while those who initially seem destructive cannot. Impulsivity and limited self-control are considered as causes of psychological disorders which can be violent or problematic.

Psychological disorders are disorders in which disturbing traits and behaviors that can disrupt people's daily functions are often disrupted and, inter alia, interfere with their adaptability. Although not an official diagnostic category, psychiatric disorders are seen as a conceptual grouping of disorders where psychiatric disorders are most common. This disorder can then be divided into two categories. For some disorders, wrong characteristics and behavior are the main symptoms listed in the diagnostic criteria for the disorder. With this disorder, problems of impulsivity and self-control (often including aggression) are seen as central aspects of basic psychopathology. In other cases, basic psychopathology may not always cause psychiatric disorders, but the nature of the disorder is usually associated with many people who have been diagnosed with the disorder.

CHAPTER ONE
DESTRUCTIVE PSYCHOLOGICAL DISORDERS

WHAT EXACTLY IS A PSYCHOLOGICAL DISORDER?

The first problem is that the psychiatrist must first decide exactly how to define "disorder". How do you determine whether something is mentally wrong or unhealthy for someone? How do you decide what is normal and what is not?

If you define disorder as something outside of statistical norms, people who are considered to be very talented or talented in a particular field are considered crazy. Rather than focusing on actions outside the normal statistical perspective, psychologists tend to focus on the outcome of that behavior. Behavior that is considered unable to adapt, causes considerable personal stress, and impaired daily functioning is more likely to be classified as a disorder.

Psychological disorders are names that are often used interchangeably with the terms psychiatric disorders, psychiatric disorders, or mental illness. The term "official" is a psychiatric disorder as defined in the latest edition of the American Psychiatric Association's Diagnostic Manual, DSM-5. It defines Psychological disorders as:

"... a syndrome characterized by clinically significant impairment of an individual's cognitive, emotional or behavioral arrangements and reflects the dysfunction of psychological, biological or developmental processes that underlie mental functions. Psychological disorders are usually associated with considerable social pressure. related, professional or other important activities. "

The DSM-5 also notes that anticipated responses to

normal stress, such as the death of a loved one, are not considered psychological disorders. Diagnostic guidelines also show that behavior that is often considered a violation of social norms is not considered a violation unless this action is based on a malfunction.

TREATMENT AND MEDICATION

From the time of Freud and Kraplin to the mid-20th century, there seemed to be only two generally accepted choices for treating patients with psychological disorders: the long-term (and especially significant) institutionalization for the most difficult and intense psychoanalysis. for those who can work outside a psychiatric clinic. The decision to persuade or take the patient to the hospital is mainly based on the level of disturbance caused by the patient to the people around them. The most destructive patients (e.g. violence) are usually sedated and it is likely that these patients will be institutionalized.

Significant developments in the past five decades have changed the profile of psychiatric care. Many people with psychological disorders have structural and functional differences in the brain. For example, Anterior Cingular Cortex dysfunction (ACC) has been identified in adolescents with psychological disorders (Gavita et al., 2012), and researchers have investigated the function and role of monoamine neurotransmitters such as serotonin and dopamine, which play a key role in the development of mental health can play game abnormalities (Malmberg et al., 2008). It is generally believed that an imbalance in activity between "hot" and "cold" brain circuits underlies many of the destructive symptoms and features. Stress hormones such as cortisol also play a role. For example, there may be a correlation between cortisol reactivity and non-emotional pulmonary nature in boys, which is common in adolescents with psychiatric disorders (Van De Wiel et al., 2004). This is in line with the current literature, which highlights the relationship between the hypothalamus-pituitary and adrenal reactivity (HPA) in stress and destructive / aggressive behavior (Stadler et al., 2011).

Because changes in the brain tend to be reflected in feelings and behavior, psychopharmacological approaches have been developed to overcome several biological factors that may be at least partially responsible for symptoms. Many of these approaches have been proven effective in reducing (and sometimes eliminating) many symptoms, including psychiatric disorders, and pharmacological interventions have been proven to be helpful, especially when symptoms are severe and potentially dangerous.

But today many critics believe that the pendulum has gone too far in the direction of pharmacological treatment. Given the increasing restrictions on drug advertising directly to consumers (the United States is one of only two countries in the world where such advertisements are permitted), advertisements for various drugs seem to fill airwaves almost every day. Radio and television stations and all drug advertisements penetrate most of the Internet. Promote a culture where treatment is seen as a better quick fix with minimal effort (if you have the right health insurance) and significant side effects that can be highlighted by many of these drugs. In addition, medicine is medicine, not medicine. When the drug is stopped, symptoms tend to return.

Many non-medical psychiatrists recognize these factors

and try to minimize pharmacological approaches rather than focusing on psychological care. Research on various forms of psychotherapy has exploded in the last five or six decades, and many specific methods for treating many specific disorders have been developed. This is a reasonable approach, especially for children and parents, because taking drugs from this group can cause unexpected reactions and medical risks. But is it realistic for psychotherapy to replace the need for psychotropic drugs? Is an increase in symptoms enough to prevent treatment?

The above questions are most important for destructive symptoms and behavior. Psychological disorders are often directed at psychological disorders (Jensen et al., 2007) and psychiatric services (Zisser & Eyberg, 2010). Most of those affected must decide whether a recommendation for a doctor or psychotherapist is sufficient. Psychological disorders, of course, require rapid stabilization because the problems experienced by the patient and those around him as a result of aggressive and impulsive actions are quite alarming and exacerbating. This shows that drug treatment can allow faster recovery. But does this mean that psychotherapy treatment is less desirable? And can benefits be maximized when combined treatment approaches (including psychological and pharmacological treatments) are used? While contributions to this book will help resolve this issue and provide much needed guidance to readers, this paper will cover a broad topic and discuss these factors, while consulting articles will help readers learn about important topics. in choosing the best treatment.

PHARMACOLOGICAL TREATMENT OF PSYCHOLOGICAL DISORDERS

Research has shown that many drugs effectively reduce symptoms and dangerous properties. Psychostimulant has been shown to reduce impulsivity (MTA Cooperative Group, 1999) while mood stabilizers - including anticonvulsants (Stanford et al. 2001), atypical antipsychotics (Buitelaar et al. 2001) and lithium (Jones et al., Serotonergic antidepressants (especially inhibitors)) : Selective serotonin reuptake or SSRIs (Coccaro et al., 2009) reduce the tendency for aggression and impulsive violence.The benefits outweigh the risks and which patients are the best candidates for treatment.

The severity of symptoms often influences the decision whether medication is needed. For example, impulsive forms or mild arousal can respond well to psychotherapy. Serious variations on these symptoms may be difficult to treat with psychological therapy, but intense and dangerous symptoms may require psychopharmacological treatment. Therefore, most doctors find that people with very limited self-control and high potential for violence generally require approaches that include pharmacological care. Jensen et al. (2007) have confirmed, for example, that the use of psychotropic drugs is usually limited to cases where symptoms are more serious and may not only respond to psychological interventions.

If psychosocial treatment is effective, gradual improvement and several sessions must be recognized. Even this decision, called "short-term therapy," usually requires 8 to 15 sessions before significant improvements can be expected. If devastating symptoms weaken the patient and pose a significant risk to those around him, it might not make sense to wait that long for improvement. Conversely, many pharmacological treatments show at least some improvement within a few days after starting treatment, although it may take several weeks (in some cases four to six) to achieve a more complete response. However, this is usually faster than psychological treatment and the rate of increase seen in treatment may be higher than the observed increase in psychotherapy during the same period.

For psychological treatment to be effective, patients must attend meetings regularly. If fast progress is needed, meetings must be held at least weekly. However, it may be difficult for some patients (or families) to go to a therapist's practice once a week and spend an hour in practice. If the patient is a child or teenager, psychotherapy must be done outside the classroom, because the absence of school one day a week to participate in psychotherapy is not practical for families or useful for students.

The cost of weekly psychotherapy can also be significant for many families, and only a few are able to get it out of their own pocket. In the United States, most patients are personally insured with health insurance that is usually purchased by employers. The quality of this layer is very different. Unfortunately, mental health care is often classified as "temporary " in the health care industry, and coverage by mental health care is often far less than medical coverage. Although federal and state laws have been passed to close this gap, there are many exceptions and the difference between medical and psychiatric treatment continues.

Limiting patient access to health care is a common way to

limit health care costs. Many people with managed health insurance have benefits that appear mainly on paper and are practically lost when the insured seeks treatment. The therapist checks the need for treatment and this check delays the session and interrupts the continuity of treatment. Initially, employees can schedule four to six sessions, and additional reviews are needed for each subsequent block. The therapist's decision is to allow further treatment. If the goalkeeper believes that the patient has made reasonable progress or that progress has not yet taken place, no further approval can be given. Although every insurance company has an appointment procedure, this appointment is internal for the insurance company and patients usually cannot be externally examined if the insurance company refuses to continue treatment. To make matters worse, meetings often take months. Meanwhile, patients remain untreated and are still at risk for themselves and those around them if devastating symptoms occur.

Another challenge is that millions of children and adolescents in the United States do not have health insurance. While the federal and state governments are trying to close this gap, there are still important parts of our society without insurance that cannot afford psychiatric care. There are a number of facilities that can treat these people, including a network of Community Mental Health Centers (CMHC) that provide care for those who need them, sometimes for free (or at least). However, in many countries CMHC has been exceeded and long waiting times (in some cases up to eight weeks) are needed before the active substance can begin treatment. Meanwhile, the patient suffers and is not treated. In rural countries, the closest CMHC may be far away. For all these reasons, patients and their families may need psychopharmacological support in lieu of additional psychosocial interventions.

PSYCHOLOGICAL TREATMENT OF PSYCHOLOGICAL DISORDERS

Although there are good reasons why pharmacology might be suitable for some patients, psychological care clearly has its place and many studies have shown that psychosocial interventions are effective. Cognitive and behavioral interventions are most clearly supported in the treatment of psychological disorders and are directly vulnerable to problematic thoughts and behaviors. Interventions that demonstrate effectiveness include training in problem solving skills (Kazdin et al., 1987b), training and problem solving skills (Kazdin et al., 1989), programs for rational mental health (Block, 2000). 1978), Triple P improved and standard (Sanders et al., 2000), anger control training (Lochman et al., 1993), group training (Huey & Rank, 1984), childhood children who were outside ordinary (Webster-Stratton & Hammond, 1997) and problem solving training for social skills (Kazdin et al., 1992). In addition, the combination of children's groups and social modeling is an effective method for raising awareness among young people with social skills about psychiatric disorders (Nash & Schaefer, 2011). Effective parent-oriented interventions include parental management training (Bernal et al., 1980; Kazdin et al., 1992), problem solving training and parental management training (Kazdin et al., 1987a), child care (Peed et al. , 1977), years of exceptional care (Webster-Stratton & Hammond, 1997), multidimensional care (both for children and caregivers; Chamberlain & Reid, 1998), multisystem therapy (for children and parents)); Henggeler et al., 1992), Parent-Child Interaction Therapy (Schuhmann et al., 1998), Parenting Barkley Learning Model (1997) Parental Children Uncontrolled (Kapalka, 2007). Similar interventions aimed at teachers have been developed, including eight steps to success in classroom management (Kapalka, 2009).

Psychological therapy can be very useful in situations where a disorder of symptoms does not seriously affect the patient or the safety of those around him. For some patients, taking medicine can be risky, which is very important for groups of patients who are vulnerable to medical or developmental consequences, e.g. Children, teenagers and parents. Most studies examining the use of psychiatric drugs last a maximum of several months, so the long-term effects of most drugs are unknown. In addition, the increase in medication usually only lasts for the time the drug is given, and the initial symptoms tend to recur when the drug is stopped. In contrast, psychosocial care gives patients new skills that apply to different life situations, and at least theoretically, these new skills are acquired more permanently. It is recommended that the therapeutic benefits of the treatment be maintained even after the therapy has ended.

Many drugs also have short-term risks and side effects. Many medications used to alleviate psychological disorders have a calming effect (at least initially, they are psychostimulants) so they can affect a patient's daily functioning and ability to work or go to school. In addition, most drugs involve other risks, including memory and concentration effects, changes in appetite and sleep patterns, cardiovascular reactions, changes in metabolism, and various other physical and psychological reactions. Although the severity of these side effects varies from person to person, it might make sense to avoid this risk and try psychological treatment first if the symptoms are not severe enough to require immediate repair.

While psycho-analysis generally requires long-term care, many psychosocial approaches today are more clearly time-limited and focus on problems. Most cognitive and behavioral treatments expect at least some progress after three or four sessions, with more significant improvements usually occurring between eight and fifteen sessions. If destructive symptoms are not too debilitating and do not pose a significant risk to the people around them, this period of time can provide adequate assistance. Because patients usually undergo psychological treatment on a regular basis, psychotherapists can usually get to know patients well. This knowledge allows professionals to monitor patient symptoms and clarify or change diagnoses when other symptoms become clear. This is very important in the context of psychological disorders, because comorbidity with other disorders is a rule and not an exception. An experienced psychiatrist can adjust the treatment to respond to all the symptoms and disorders that occur during the treatment.

For patients with good health insurance, the cost of psychotherapy can only cover payments (especially when using network operators), which limits costs. Non-health service providers can be candidates for various forms of free or subsidized support offered by federal, state and local government agencies, as well as various non-profit organizations. Although the availability of these programs varies greatly from country to country (and often from section to section), patients in some parts of the country may have access to this service.

COMBINED TREATMENT OF PSYCHOLOGICAL AND MENTAL DISORDERS

It is clear that every modality, pharmacotherapy and psychological treatment offers unique benefits that overcome or minimize inherent problems when the approach is used as monotherapy. Medication only works as long as it is given, but psychological care offers constant change and new skills. Drugs can cause side effects, the use of psychotherapy can (at least theoretically) allow lower drug doses, and combination treatment has the added advantage that more frequent drug reactions (including side effects and desires) are monitored by psychotherapists seeing their patients more often than doctor's prescription. For example, psychotherapists can overcome other problems related to drug use.

Researchers are increasingly investigating the integration of psychotherapy and psychopharmacology as a means of treating various psychiatric disorders (Kutcher et al., 2004). Indeed, psychiatric disorders are the most commonly reported psychiatric disorders (Jensen et al., 2007), and many of these recommendations come from non-medical psychologists, suggesting that many professionals seek joint treatment for their patients. Look for this integrative approach that allows simultaneous treatment of biological, behavioral, cognitive, and psychosocial aspects of this disorder.

However, an integrative approach to the treatment of psychological disorders is rarely examined. The lack of results from this study is challenging for doctors because there are several guidelines for integrating treatment.

Although it makes sense that the combination of the two therapies maximizes therapeutic benefits, the added validity of adding one treatment to another is rarely explored, and in some cases the results are inconsistent when the combination is examined. On the one hand, the results show that the combination of psychotherapy and pharmacotherapy is superior to a single treatment of mood and personality disorders (Kool et al., 2007). On the other hand, the increased Attention Deficit Hyperactivity Disorder (ADHD) for combination therapy or monotherapy with psycho-stimulant does not differ significantly from behavioral therapy alone (MTA Cooperative Group, 1999). But statistically, only joint interventions are greater than the symptoms of oppositional. It is therefore clear that increasing the validity of adding one treatment to another is not yet known, and doctors currently have no reason to judge how far further improvements can be expected when one treatment is added to another.

The right combination of care settings is also largely unexplored. Many believe that, except in very severe cases, the initial treatment for most patients must be cognitive, or behavioral therapy should only add medication if the improvement is not enough. Conversely, reverse order can also have advantages. Stabilizing the initial symptoms can increase participation in psychotherapy and subsequently increase the therapeutic benefits. Therefore, when considering combination therapy, the question of which modality to use is not answered.

The method of integrating the two therapies is also unknown. Are lower drug doses needed if the patient is treated psychosocially at the same time? Are less intensive (and less common) psychological treatments used when using drugs? Not only do these questions remain unanswered, but it is also possible that the answers to these questions vary depending on the characteristics of the patient and the patient's reaction to individual modalities. Therefore, doctors must assess various aspects of this problem themselves.

Access to combination drugs can also be a big challenge. Ideally, a psychiatrist will do both treatments. In the United States, however, the use of drugs and psychotherapy is very different because some specialists offer both therapies. Although practicing psychiatrists and psychiatric nurses at least theoretically completes psychotherapy training, only a few actually offer this service and most only deal with drug management. In addition, the United States suffers from a significant shortage of psychiatric doctors, which is why most psychotropic prescriptions are written by general practitioners, internists, and pediatricians who have no training (or time) to provide psychological care. In contrast, non-medical psychiatrists cannot prescribe medication. An exception is that some psychologists have received extensive medical training and two states (New Mexico and Louisiana), US territories in Guam, and various branches of the US government have authorized these psychologists to prescribe psychotropic drugs. To date, around 150 psychologists with this training have prescribed medicine, and the number is increasing. For example, Illinois has just issued regulations for trained psychologists. However, 150 providers that can offer combined treatment are not enough to meet the demand, which is why patients who need both treatments will usually need services from two mental health providers at least in the near future. This not only consumes time and financial resources, but also raises questions about access to care, especially in rural areas with few psychiatric professionals.

Finally, practitioners who consider whether to use pharmacotherapy, psychotherapy, or both treatments must make a decision that considers various aspects of this case, and the choice can vary. The advantages and challenges of treating psychological disorders from one patient to another. The following guidelines can help practitioners make such decisions.

CLINICAL POINTS

Pharmacotherapy as monotherapy can provide easier access (because health care providers are more common, especially in rural areas) and can be cheaper and more time-consuming. On the other hand, drugs are just drugs, not drugs, and symptoms tend to return when the drug is stopped.

Different categories of psychotropic drugs are used to treat psychological disorders, and the risks and side effects are very different. While SSRIs generally tolerate psycho-stimulants and anti-depressants well, mood stabilizers and atypical antipsychotics generally have more significant side effects and higher medical risks.

The use of drugs has not been studied in the long term, so the long-term risks and side effects are unknown. This mainly affects vulnerable groups of patients, including children, adolescents and the elderly. Most psychiatric drugs are also associated with significant risks during pregnancy. In these patients, the use of psychological interventions is usually considered the first approach.

Psychological care is less risky and can offer additional benefits from long-term improvement, because changes and nursing skills can persist after treatment is stopped.

On the other hand, improvement is usually gradual and usually requires at least a few sessions for real change, with 15 or more sessions required for complete results. Access to suppliers may be difficult, especially in remote and rural areas, especially those who have been trained in the best practices discussed here.

The choice of treatment is often very much determined by the severity of the symptoms. Patients with the most severe symptoms, especially when these symptoms threaten others, stabilize more quickly with drugs.

At least combination therapy can offer benefits from each of its modalities, although this is not strongly supported by available clinical trials.

An important consideration is the added value when one treatment is added to another. The doctor must consider how much further improvement is possible after the second treatment. Doctors need to consider the added value of more time and resources when using two providers and accessing both types of providers.

Adherence to psychiatric medications can be inconsistent, especially if they have significant side effects that excite patients (such as sedation, memory problems, sexual dysfunction, etc.). In some cases, combination treatment allows doctors to improve drug monitoring and respond to concerns and side effects because both providers can monitor patient responses to drugs.

With combination therapy, both providers must maintain close contact. Both providers must maintain and promote both therapies. Patients must receive messages from both providers, resulting in a maximum increase in additional contributions from both therapies.

The doctor must identify and review the preferences of patients and family members for each modality. Clinicians must also accept that the modality in which patients and their families express their clearest preferences will most likely be followed and will ultimately lead to the greatest response. Combination therapy is most likely effective if the patient accepts that both therapies are needed to reduce symptoms optimally.

CHAPTER TWO
THE STRUCTURE AND FUNCTION OF THE BRAIN DURING IMPULSIVENESS AND PSYCHOLOGICAL DISORDERS

Usually people consider themselves "above the animal kingdom," which is mainly due to the development (sophistication) of the human brain. A significant increase in the size and complexity of the cerebral cortex compared with the rest of the brain has enabled humans to maintain a healthy balance or homeostasis in many areas at the same time. "Lower" (subcortical) regions in the brain are controlled by inhibitory control.

Although this view is too simple, the function hierarchy is very helpful for understanding human behavior, especially when the problem of behavior becomes a problem for people or society. For example, the Orbitofrontal Cortex (OFC) and its relationship to the lower brain region are related to controlling social behavior and monitoring reactive aggression, because an accidental explosion blows up this part of the brain from Phineas Gage (Brodal, 2010). Problems manifest themselves openly through interventions in self control, impulse control or through psychological disorders.

This chapter tries to analyze the complexity of psychological disorders by summarizing neurobiological findings in two areas: impulsivity / self control and aggression. This concludes with a brief summary of the diseases most affected by this area. First, a brief review and review of relevant neurobiological concepts and terms helps to determine the context.

IMPORTANT BRAIN REGIONS AND NEUROTRANSMITTERS
Although the metaphors are very simple, they resemble

complex and interconnected nervous system wiring, which is often the most effective explanation for patients. In this metaphor, the brain consists of several "nodes" and "wires" connected by wires, each of which plays a role in various aspects of behavior. In the example of Phineas Gage above, OFC is a node that plays a role in integrating emotional behavior and providing information about emotional decisions (Fuster, 2008).

Other areas of the brain (and some of their roles) that are relevant to the discussion in this chapter include: the Anterior Cingular Cortex (ACC; regulating / initiating targeted behavior, monitoring processes, recognizing / focusing on mistakes, choosing behavior))) in the event of a conflict duty); Ventromedial Prefrontal Cortex (VMPFC; emotional memory for limbic regulation; suppression of premature actions); Dorsolateral Prefrontal Cortex (DLPFC; planning, working memory, cognitive flexibility); lower frontal cortex (IFC; inhibits motor reactions, cognitive changes, selective and persistent attention; Fuster, 2008); Basal ganglia (motor training, behavioral automation); Amygdala (emotional coloring from learned experiences, emotional fear, conditioned fear); and ventral striatum / nuclear insight (emotional components of motivation, positive emotions, appreciation; Brodal, 2010).

Unlike the cables that transmit electricity through our homes, relatively few brain neurons "light up". Conversely, neuron connections are closer to the "joints", where gaps - or synapses - show areas of neurotransmitter traffic that represent the flow of information. Most importantly, many drugs have the greatest impact on the level of synapses and neurotransmitters.

Of the various synapses that occupy the focal sensor system, dopamine, serotonin, and norepinephrine are the main players in this account. Each of these particles has different functions in the brain and along the way, depending on whether it is connected to several receptors through which it transmits data. Dopamine is associated with meetings with gifts, inspiration, attention, motor control and learning. Serotonin with temperament, calm, hungry, sexual behavior and learning; and norepinephrine with excitement, social relations and rest (Fogel and Kapalka, 2012). In terms of focus on this section, dopamine is the most significant of the three, according to the research reported.

At the level of the most complex neurons, the results of message correspondence depend on the temporary and spatial addition of inhibitory and excitatory improvements. The dominance of information sources that inhibit the flow of data guide. A comparable procedure manages the movement of the end-to-end system, an inhibiting pathway that controls the removal of areas of the brain efficiently, provided it is not overcome by recording excitatory information (Fogel and Kapalka, 2012).

Sources of information that appear to influence current behavior depend on whether they appear faster than controversial news. The faster or more significant the endurance of the behavior, the more likely the nervous system will be depressed and thus out of control. Basal ganglia in particular do the most convincing job of getting a programmed exercise machine. The "neural races" model is proposed

Research has long focused on the subcortical pathways underlying "race" between being invited to participate or end an activity (Schmidt et al., 2013). At the risk of reusing frames, this thinking works well. Neural "internal conflicts" occur when a person is seen with a number of activities.

Many codes of ethics, which include activities and organized guidance through criticism, use a chain or circle between the frontal cortex and the shell zone (Swamp et al., 2009). Specifically, the prefrontal cortical area extends parallel to the basal ganglia, at this point to the midbrain, the thalamus and back to the cortex. Errors or damage to this system are responsible for a number of overpayments, including over-the-counter problems, Tourette, and ADHD.

Some analysts describe various forms of social manifestations that result from official "cold" or "hot" capacities associated with basic neural hardware (Rubia, 2011). In this situation, "heat" indicates the extent to which inspirational or eager power is involved, no one is considered autonomous. Again, these synopsis ideas are redefined excessively, but they are somehow useful as logical devices, especially when using differential determinations. While ADHD is regularly seen as a "cold" problem with manifestations reflecting intellectual dysregulation, the extent to which a person experiences fractures in the limbic region (amygdala, ventral striatum) or corticolimbic (OFC, VMPFC) to provide additional evidence of enthusiastic dysregulation (Shaw et al., 2014). Such cases can be a symptomatic problem, but can be clearly explained in terms of standards and neurobiological findings.

IMPULSIVE BEHAVIOR

Pulses and nerve researchers have long believed that this phenomenon is a multifactorial design that encompasses a variety of behaviors such as hyperexcitability, disinhibition, low sensitivity to side effects, rapid response before proper planning, and minimal concern for long-term effects (Moeller et al., 2001) to see life problems caused by this behavior.

General characteristics of impulsive behavior phenomena distinguish choices from actions (Winstanley et al., 2006). Impulsive decisions reflect skewed judgments about the consequences and preferences for immediate or late rewards, even though they recognize that future rewards are greater. Conversely, impulsive actions reflect a failure to inhibit responses - the ability to inhibit responses that have a strong (dominant) impulse (Reynolds et al., 2006). Part of the power in categorizing impulsivity using these two broad concepts rests on neuroanatomical evidence of common and different neurobiological pathways that modulate impulse decisions and impulse effects (Chambers et al., 2009). Note that animal behavior is rather one-sided in both cases: instant appreciation and minimal oppression. Instead, parents are expected to consider late satisfaction and prevent inappropriate reactions in certain contexts.

Deferring a discount or avoiding a delay is related to preferences for instant prizes. However, this is only clinically relevant if later rewards are higher. People who are described as impulsive tend to postpone their concessions (Kirby et al., 1999). This is a normative feature of children, but becomes problematic and exaggerated in the case of ADHD, an impulsive disorder which is characteristic of adolescents (Sonuga-Barke, 2005). Defining the boundary between normal and abnormal in this area is an ongoing problem that reflects broader psychiatric and psychiatric problems that neurobiology cannot yet overcome.

In children with ADHD, delay difficulties can be more serious than the terms "discount" and "avoidance". Time

(Wilbertz et al., 2013).

NEUROBIOLOGICAL FACTORS THAT CONTRIBUTE TO IMPULSIVITY

Investigation of nerve impulse substrates is said to inhibit reactions. There is increased activity in the prefrontal cortex when adolescents perform tasks that require behavioral suppression (Marsh et al., 2006). With regard to the time associated with delayed selection, VMPFC is activated selectively in direct calls, whereas a longer delay triggers DLPFC (McClure et al., 2004). This finding shows that choice is directly related to more emotional reactions. The results are also relatively good with respect to reduced activity in the striatum and in the ACC (Tamm et al., 2004). The whole sequence of behavioral combinations of functional models is problematic because children adopt unplanned behavior without being able to delay assignments if necessary.

Apart from the front, wages have been shown to play a role in various aspects of impulse management. Most impulsive decisions are reward pathways that seem to track the subjective value of prizes regardless of whether they are delayed or not (Monterosso & Luo, 2010). Ventral striatum is reduced in response to inhibition of response and expectation of administration (Carmona et al., 2011). The caudal cores and amygdala increase the delay in administration activity (Plichta et al., 2009). The ventricular striatal and limbic areas are reduced during motivational control efforts (Cubillo et al., 2012). The general conclusion that can be drawn from this research is that delaying gifts, controlling behavior, and inhibiting violent reactions is considered disgusting (can be called "unnatural").

For example, several different brain regions contribute to behavioral suppression, but convergent evidence suggests that IFC, especially in the right hemisphere, is a common space in many targeted behavioral studies (Dodds et al., 2011). In addition, two circuits appear to be very impulsive (Grant & Kim, 2013): distributor circuits and motor control circuits involved in inhibition reactions. The former seems to be modulated by dopamine and serotonin, while the latter is more modulated by noradrenaline (Grant & Kim, 2013).

Researchers have provided evidence about the involvement of the dopaminergic system in impulsivity through specific variants of the ADHD gene and receptor transport (Baumgaertel et al., 2008). Dopamine plays a key role in developing and continuing the function of the front circuit, based on the value of decision making and the ability to delay gifts (Volkow et al., 2009). The manifestation of selection or switching to alternatives is related to the dopaminergic phase of the "plague" (Oades, 1985), which links reward pathways with impulsive decisions. At the same time, dopamine supports the attention process and focuses on important aspects of the environment (Rubia et al., 2009).

Research consistently shows a direct inverse relationship between impulse behavior and serotonin levels (Moeller et al., 2001). Extensive studies also show the role of serotonin in various aspects of ADHD, with the potential for differences between impulsive, careless dominant, and hyperactive dominant types (Oades, 2008). Given the number and variations of serotonin receptors, some of which have opposite effects (Fineberg et al., 2014), the relationship between impulsive behavior and serotonergic clay is very complex. In addition, serotonergic and dopaminergic effects are related to manifestations and behavioral control, but these interactions have not been examined in detail compared to individual signaling pathways (Oades, 2008).

AGGRESSIVENESS

Like impulsivity which is not uniform, aggression denies a simple definition. In many cases, aggression can be observed between planned, proactive or instrumental on the one hand and impulsive, affective or reactive on the other. A common theme for the first type is goal-directed behavior, similar to predatory behavior that is usually not caused by seizures.

Conversely, impulsive aggression usually manifests itself in response to perceived stress that affects the autonomic nervous system and the emotional processing centers of the brain (Siever, 2008).

NEUROBIOLOGICAL FACTORS THAT CONTRIBUTE TO AGGRESSIVENESS

Environmental and historical factors play an important role in developing trends for reactive or impulsive aggression, especially early physical violence, inconsistent parents, or reduced parental supervision (Patterson et al., 2000). But also with the strong influence of parents on children's behavior, differences in children's behavior can be explained by reactions to the genetic temperament underlying children (Larsson et al., 2008). However, these results highlight a strong contrast with proactive aggression, which in longitudinal studies is largely mediated by genetic factors (Tuvblad et al., 2009).

In the field of impulsive aggression, one of the more consistent findings leads to the fact that low serotonin levels are associated with an increased likelihood of aggressive behavior - the most obvious of which is total suicide - although the binding of different serotonin receptors has the opposite effect (Seaver, 2008). For example, the effects of serotonin on aggressive behavior in people with ADHD (Flory et al., 2007) and repeated blast disorder (IED; Coccaro & McCloskey, 2010), especially in the limbic region, have been well documented.

If frustration is related to the negative effects of impulsive solutions that reach a certain threshold, this can lead to aggression. For example, adolescents who are classified as aggressive already have relatively low levels of serotonin. When faced with the task of inhibiting reactions that further decrease serotonin levels, they are more likely to be impulsive and aggressive (LeMarquand et al., 1998).

The limbic structure reacts behaviorally to the streets through the lower central nervous system with impulsive aggression. Prefrontal Cortical areas - such as the medial OFC, Anterior Insula and ACC - send inhibitory connections to modulate this emotional expression. For example the neural race described above, it has been found that people who respond to impulsive aggression have excessive limbic activity, dysfunction in areas that inhibit the brain, or low serotonergic tones (New et al., 2002).

On the other hand, instrumental aggression in adolescents is associated with the subsequent development of psychopathic traits (Pardini & Frick, 2013). A common theme of various findings is the reduction of physiological arousal and activity at the center of emotional processing (Siever, 2008). Reduced amygdala activity in response to negative emotions in others indicates that antisocial behavior tends to lead to goals (Passamonti et al., 2010).

This finding is also in line with the decrease in the possibility of an increase in therapy (Pardini & Frick, 2013). In contrast to reactive aggression, no serotonin levels are detected. However, some results suggest a possible role in reducing norepinephrine levels, which is associated with hostile signal responses (Stedler et al., 2010).

PSYCHOPATHOLOGY

Impulsivity and aggression are divided into various categories of psychiatric disorders, including personality disorders, mood disorders, psychiatric disorders, and substance abuse disorders. In the latest issue of the American Psychiatric Association (APA), 2013, Guide to Diagnosis and Statistics on Psychological Disorders, one of the many changes from the previous edition, including the reorganization of the Psychological Disorders section. One of the organizational principles explicitly mentioned by the DSM-5 working group in its initial discussion (Charney et al., 2002) is the alignment of criteria and diagnostic groups along neurobiological pathways.

Although a reliable diagnostic classification of neurobiological substrates requires further research, DSM-5 seems to be successful in several ways when considering the difference between psychiatric disorders (Clark et al., 2000). The fourth edition of the ADHD manual (DSM-IV-TR) summarizes oppositional disruptive Disorder (ODD) and behavior disorder due to external behavior problems (APA, 2000) and separates them from other disorders. impulse control. In contrast, DSM-5 divides ADHD into its own category and highlights the aggression that underlies the last two diagnoses.

Psychological disorders are believed to be related to the nature of the underlying psychopathology, and convergence of evidence suggests common genetic factors (Arcos-Burgos et al., 2012). A study examining the genetic and environmental effects of the development of psychological disorders has shown a significant impact on the history of drug use and antisocial personality disorder in the elderly (Dick et al., 2005). Instead of distinguishing between certain genetic factors that show the inherited relationship between child abuse and certain antisocial personality disorders and psychological disorders, a "shared responsibility" is proposed which makes children vulnerable to the development of subsequent behavioral problems. (Bornalova et al., 2010).

ATTENTION DEFICIT HYPERACTIVITY DISORDER ADHD

Much time and resources have been spent identifying the neurobiological substrate of ADHD. The lack of consistent evidence generally confirms some people's view that ADHD is "not a real disorder". However, a more plausible explanation reflects the heterogeneity of the disorder (Baumgaertel et al., 2008). The most commonly reported structural volume reductions in ADHD are the forehead, basal ganglia, and brain stem (Valera et al., 2007).

Comparison of healthy controls for adolescents with ADHD highlights the cool role of EF forefront in mediating attention (Rubia, 2011). Study of nerve pathways shows deficits in the relationship between the frontal region and the striatum, cingulum, parietal lobe and cerebellum, and between the parietal lobe and back lobe (Konrad & Eickhoff, 2010). Specifically, as mentioned above, IFC (Dodds et al., 2011) is the most common specific prefrontal area in ADHD imaging studies. Therefore, deactivating IFC can act as a biomarker for the disorder.

Further evidence shows an ineffective relationship

between the amygdala and AFF in children with ADHD (Plessen et al., 2006), which can explain the poor cortical self-regulation of amygdala-mediated emotional processes, especially those related to delayed retention. Behavioral manifestations of this lack of self-regulation can begin to look like ODD or even CD (Rubia et al., 2009). These findings are relatively common considering the level of comorbidity in the disease.

In general, brain vessel volume is associated with ADHD symptoms and a thorough analysis of brain structures, especially the upper brain (Mackie et al., 2007). While the cerebellum is assigned several functions outside motor coordination, the perception of time in an impulsive context is of special interest (Nigg & Casey, 2005). A common theme that links the various behavioral problems that characterize children with ADHD is that it is difficult to act in a timely or effective manner.

A consistent finding in the ADHD literature is a change in the function and presence of norepinephrine and dopamine (Baumgaertel et al., 2008). In general, norepinephrine modulates inhibitory control through the IFC network, whereas delayed selection is more OFC and is modulated by dopamine (Fineberg et al., 2014). Their circuit function in particular requires a balanced level of these two neurotransmitters. Prefrontal cortical function can be impaired by overuse (e.g. shown in bipolar disorder) or inadequate (e.g. demonstrated in ADHD) dopamine or stimulation of norepinephrine receptors (Arnsten, 2006).

One way of link design is modulation and switching of signals and noise, with noradrenaline activity associated with the first activity and dopamine activity associated with the second activity (Oades, 1985). Noradrenaline acts as a stimulator in ventromedial stimulation as well as in the lateral prefrontal region and stimulates the attention system (Arnsten, 2006). When environmental pollution increases and the autonomic nervous system is triggered, norepinephrine levels increase, arousal levels increase and attention is disturbed. Basal dopamine levels are also needed to activate certain environmental stimuli. if not, pay attention "traffic". However, excess dopamine causes an unstable focus (Arnsten, 2006). In this context, stimulants fight ADHD symptoms, strengthen signaling information and help "smooth out" excessive noise, but only if the dose is in the correct range (Arnsten, 2006).

CONFLICTING OPPOSITIONAL DISRUPTIVE AND INTERFERENCE

Oppositional disruptive and contradictory disorders as diagnostic disorders are relatively rare and always appear as comorbidities, often with other psychiatric disorders (Greene, 2006). For this reason, there are only limited studies on "clean" diseases, especially from a neurobiological point of view. Some imagine that ODD is characterized by negative rather than impulsive emotions (APA, 2013), which shows the involvement of limbic circuits. A recent study of prefunctional neurovascular function on neuronal correlations of inhibitory control in pure ODD shows reduced right IFC activation (Zhu et al., 2014), which is in line with other studies of impulse control, but increased activation in regions near each other suggested that such behavior might be the result of connections between them. However, the results are not stable and research is limited by the small sample size. Overall, ODD appears to be less stressful and less prominent with respect to ADHD and CD, and limited research to date seems to support the World Health Organization's (1992) approach to treating ODD as a softer CD subtype (Stedler et al., 2010),

CONDUCT DISORDER

Neurological development theory is used to differentiate CDs and adolescent children based on different biological vulnerabilities to the first and social causes in the latter (Moffitt, 1993). However, research has identified structural anomalies that are believed to contribute to behavioral problems regardless of human age (Fairchild et al., 2011). Recent efforts to explain the path of CD development have focused on non-emotional (CU) harmless nature (Pardini & Frick, 2013). CU's properties are becoming increasingly important as CD trademarks for various reasons. The prevalence is not only significant (10% -50%; Kahn et al., 2012), but the longitudinal clinical effects are more severe than in adolescents without these characteristics. The early CD development pathway, which is characterized by serious anger management problems, underlines the close relationship with ODD as an existing syndrome.

The high incidence of comorbidity between CD and ADHD complicates the analysis of the neurobiological signaling pathways underlying each disorder (Rubia, 2011). However, it is possible to distinguish ADHD from CD because of the differences between these networks in terms of specific executive functions. As noted above, ADHD is characterized by a lack of cold EF pathways, which leads to a reduction in resistance to downstream reactions and attention control. On the other hand, CD includes the deactivation of the thermal EF cortical structure (ACC) in the regulation of subcortical structures (amygdala), which provides motivation and influence (Decety et al., 2009).

TIC DISORDER

By definition, tic disorders are movement disorders and therefore also include nerve pathways. Most studies identify the striatum as "the main pathophysiological site of Tourette's syndrome" (Harris & Singer, 2006, p. 679) and emphasize the role of Corticostriatal-thalamic-cortical (CSTC) stings in the expression and suppression of tic. (Marsh et al., 2009). Intervention in the striatum / basal ganglia is the heart of automatic behavior. In addition to DLPFC, the basal ganglia and thalamus components of this chain, tic can be caused by regulatory disorders in other brain areas, including the brain and insula (Towbin, 2009). Their role in this disorder is less clear and consistent, but they may be related to sensory perceptions that accompany the experience (Marsh et al., 2009).

In terms of neurochemistry, several neurotransmitters seem to affect tic disorders, with dopaminergic pathways being most affected (Towbin, 2009). This is in line with the well-known role of dopamine not only in modulating all stages of the CSTC motorcycle, but also in motivation and attention. The proposed mechanism by which tic overcome suppression reflects the detection of dual dopamine release (tonic phase) at synapses. Research supports the possibility of (early) release of low tonnage and an increase in "blast" phase or rate to explain the occurrence of tic (Harris & Singer, 2006).

Aside from the peculiar nature of some tic, especially the complicated ones, this disorder can be diagnostic confusing because the behavior is not entirely unintentional (APA, 2013). Is this impulsive behavior? The subjective feeling of the tic group seems to be comparable to other impulse control disorders. This apparent confusion is removed when considering the neural pathways mentioned that reflect different versions of the balance between the "higher" and "lower" centers. While DLPFC and other prefrontal areas are active, tic tend to suffocate (Marsh et al., 2009). However, increased stress or emotional intensity is associated with an increase in the frequency and intensity of tic (Towbin, 2009), which shows a stronger subcutaneous effect.

Although aggression is usually not associated with flea disorders, people with chronic tic or Tourette's disorders may have aggressive, impulsive, or other psychiatric disorders as part of the symptom picture (Towbin, 2009). These additional behavioral problems are more likely to occur when diagnosing comorbidities, especially with ADHD. Basic neurobiological details have not yet been completed, but participation in the CSTC chain is very possible. The DLPFC chain is involved in ADHD and Tourette comorbidities because of its role in management functions (Wright et al., 2012).

INTERMITTENT EXPLOSIVE DISORDER

Intermittent explosive disorders are usually a diagnosis to rule out other clinical causes of the angry explosive situation that characterizes the presentation (APA, 2013). However, "mild signs" of neurological disorders can underlie this disorder. As can be seen from the description of DSM-5, IED further aggravates the problem of self-control due to emotional dysregulation (APA, 2013). In addition, IEDs are associated with negative feelings or consequences, which indicate that aggressive behavior is impulsive. There is a bug in the top-down path in controlling the effects of overcharging. On the one hand, this is one of the clearest examples of "thermal problems" associated with neurobiological functions. For example, patients with IED increase amygdala activity and decrease OFC activity when they see angry faces (Coccaro & McCloskey, 2010).

BIPOLAR DISORDER

The neurobiological basis of bipolar disorder (BD) is still inconclusive, although the results of the study reveal some common problems. The complexity of this disorder is reflected in the series of neurotransmitters and signaling pathways that lead to functional disorders of symptoms. Like the other disorders described in this chapter, the theme of repetitive balance between prefrontal and subcortical regions concerns BD, but the pathological manifestations of this imbalance are emotional dysregulation and mood disorders.

Impulsive behavior is a delusional characteristic and can be very problematic because of the increased risk of suicide (APA, 2013). Neurovisual studies have shown that impulsivity is a trait similar to BD (Trost et al., 2014). OFC is a prefrontal area that has received the most empirical support for involvement in suicidal behavior in BD (Mahon et al., 2012). The relationship of OFC with the amygdala, basal ganglia, ACC, and temporal lobes underscores its role in decision making, impulse control, and regulation of emotional expression. Extensive studies have found abnormal size and function of OFC in BD (Mahon et al., 2012). In addition, Trost et al. (2014) found evidence of problems with ventral prefrontal striatum regulation which reduces the ability of BD patients to delay long-term responses.

Children diagnosed with BD and comorbid psychological disorders have an increased risk of aggressive behavior (Kohn & Asnis, 2003). In contrast to the findings of decreased amygdala activity in adolescents with CD with CU features, children with BD show an increase in amygdala response to neutral facial images (Rich et al., 2006). Therefore, their aggression is more reactive or affective than instrumental. Aggressive behavior in BD tends to manifest itself in a mixed state (not manic or depressed) caused by greater disorganization in the limbic region (Kohn & Asnis, 2003).

PERSONALITY DISORDER

Impulsive and emotional behavior reactions, which are usually associated with negative interpersonal effects, are a major feature of personality disorders in Cluster B (PD). Two of these disorders, Antisocial Personality Disorder and Borderline Personality Disorder (BPD), are the only ones that include impulsivity and aggressiveness in diagnostic criteria (APA, 2013).

Personality disorders are generally not considered "neurobiological" in terms of conceptualization and treatment, but some traits are more conditioned than neural networks or neurotransmitter pathways. There is also plenty of evidence linking young people and adults with children's temperament (Clonninger & Svrakic, 2000). Temperament is basically not negative, but can cause boredom, impulsivity, and anger outbursts, followed by psychological disorders and interpersonal problems.

Impulsive behavior is related to the severity of PSA, but not to the choice of impulse (Swann et al., 2009). Due to adolescent brains with behavioral disorders, structural imaging studies of HPE nerve correlation have identified an important role for the prefrontal cortex, especially for OFC (Huebner et al., 2008). Other fields of interest include the amygdala, insula and striatum (Passamonti et al., 2010). Problems with the prefrontal cortex-hippocampus relationship in adults with LPS can explain the inability to learn from experience, especially contextual evidence, and can cause impulsive responses with little or no bite (Getz, 2014). This combination of results underscores the EF hot track structure and development from CD to PPE (Rubia, 2011). For example, when healthy controls see images of intentional or unintentional damage, they show a stronger relationship between VMPFC and amygdala, which shows control reactions with strong side effects (Decety et al., 2009). In contrast, adolescents with a history of severe aggressive behavior show a far more intense response in limbic and somatosensory brain regions without activation and prefrontal connectivity, which shows modulation of behavior through negative effects.

In BPD patients, emotional dysregulation is a characteristic that often manifests itself as impulsive aggression (APA, 2013). Although some details are still known, neurobiological findings have consistently demonstrated anterior limbic dysfunction, especially in tissues such as ACC, OFC, DLPFC, amygdala and hippocampus (Leichsenring et al., 2011). In particular, excessive amygdala activation in response to emotional triggers coincides with decreased prefrontal activation, which is therefore not enough to control the increase in emotional responses. The results are usually unstable or messy. Impulsivity and instability that become aggressive are mainly related to disrupted OFC activity (Getz, 2014).

OTHER DESTRUCTIVE PSYCHOLOGICAL DISORDERS

Other clinical disorders can be characterized by aggressive or impulsive episodes, although the symptoms are not always prototypical. For example, aggressive and impulsive behavior related to delirium, dementia, and substance-related disorders (APA, 2013). The extent to which such behavior is observed in this disorder is generally seen in neurological or neuropsychological assessments. The results are almost always the same as most of this chapter. Patients with Alzheimer's dementia who have behavioral disorders, for example, show decreased activity in OFC, DLPFC and ACC compared to patients with Alzheimer's disease, without obvious behavioral problems (Lane et al., 2011).

The increased likelihood of psychiatric disorders in developmental disorders such as psychiatric disorders or autism spectrum disorders reflects a lack of more general or more diffuse neurological functions (Lecavalier et al., 2011). This is reflected in differences in imaging and neurochemical studies (Getz, 2014). While impulsivity and aggression are not considered to be the main characteristics of developmental disorders, such behavior can explode in isolated cases, apparently "from the start".

Psychiatrists face a daunting but central task to draw a line between normal and abnormal behavior. Behaviors such as impulsivity and aggression seem to be relatively clear on the "abnormal" side of the fence. However, this behavior must be contextually socially, culturally, and generally evolutionary. People worry about inhibiting response, delayed gratification, and long-term planning unless they are compatible with other species, which are expressions of complex cortical control. But it is clear that some moments require "animal responses" such as racing, creative arts, and romantic relationships. This trend is always balanced and has different neurobiological characteristics.

When treating people with impulse control, psychological disorders or aggression, it is important to maintain balance when making treatment decisions. This chapter discusses aspects of psychological disorders that have a more significant biological etiology. Of these, ADHD, bipolar, IED, and tic disorders seem to depend most on their physiological origin, which is reflected in their treatment protocol. On the other hand, studies of the etiology of ODD, CD, and antisocial personality disorders and limitations are more definitive. Therefore, doctors are more likely to give instructions to clients in psychological care, except in the most serious cases.

CHAPTER THREE
DEVELOPMENT OF IMPULSIVENESS AND PSYCHOLOGICAL DISORDERS

Disorders of adaptive prosocial behavior usually occur with poor pulse modulation and emotional dysregulation (Arsenio & Lemerise, 2010). There are several ways in which impulse control can cause behavioral disorders. For example, some people have problems controlling normal impulse ranges (such as Attention Deficit Hyperactivity Disorder or ADHD), while others have extreme impulses that exceed the expected range (such as repeated explosive disorders). and some may have a combination of both (as seen with tic disorders). Driving that interferes with poor modulation and limited emotional regulation (e.g. anger and low tolerance for frustration) affects one's ability to regulate one's own behavior, which is a major component of psychological disorders.

The level of self-control and aggression is known as the basic dimension of psychological disorders (Broidy et al., 2003), based on the assumption that psychological disorders are the product of failure of self-control, the expression of aggressive behavior, that is, aggressive behavior or a combination of aggression and limited self-control. To understand the psychological aspects of psychological disorders, an examination of the development of self-control and aggression is needed.

Self control

Many social scientists have defined self-control as a measure that can be used to fight impulses, suppress impulses or overcome them and delay gratification (Vazsonyi & Huang, 2010). Gailliot et al. (2007) also describe self-control as part of individual personalities, which allows them to suppress thoughts, feelings, and behaviors to maximize rewards and respect cultural norms. People who are able to control themselves adequately can improve their goals and achieve desired results, including social acceptance, interpersonal growth, cognitive stability and personal, professional and academic outcomes.

Conversely, irregular self-control can be associated with a series of disturbed cognitive expressions such as inattention or distraction, or can be expressed through irregular behavior such as hyperactivity and tics. Problems with executive functioning (language, memory and planning) can also be related to these difficulties (Barkley, 1997; Fischer et al., 1990). In general, destructive impulses occur and the spectrum of psychological disorders can vary greatly. Only a small portion of the population has limited self-control, so the diagnostic burden of psychological disorders becomes clear.

Life development perspective illuminates the acquisition and progress of self-control and its relationship with psychological disorders. Self-control is usually seen in the first year of life and gradually increases from year to year from small children to early childhood (Barkley, 1997). This developmental sequence is directly related to language, memory and attention, all of which developed simultaneously during the founding years (Berk, 2008). Supported or inhibited by environmental influences and psychosocial development, self-control in the development of puberty remains relatively stable until adulthood (Broidy et al., 2003).

It is important to recognize the role played by individual differences in the acquisition and development of self-control. According to Vazsonyi and Huang (2010), some differences can be expected in children, although many factors contribute to the development and development of self-regulation and this may be caused by innate trends. Differences in emotional regulation, coping strategies, conscious effort, motivation and personal relationships can mediate the integration of self-control as prosocial behavior (Gilliom et al., 2002). According to Barkley (1997) "individual differences in inhibition seem to determine for greater effectiveness in tasks with delayed reactions or for general developmental levels" (p. 210). In addition to inherent differences, however, etiology and the development of lifelong self-control are explained in cognitive, behavioral, and social learning models.

INTRAPERSONAL FACTORS THAT AFFECT SELF CONTROL

Cognitive and behavioral perspectives complement our understanding of the pathogenesis of psychological disorders through self-control disorders. In the original self-control study, Russell Barkley (1997) formulated self-control as an individual's self-directed cognitive behavioral response to inhibit weak responses over a substantial period of time, thereby increasing the likelihood of desired goals. Modern theoretical models for social learning also emphasize the role of strong knowledge; Individuals not only react to environmental stimuli, but also individuals who are active, receptive and wise to their environment (Bandura, 1977). Cognitive behavioral problems such as tolerance of frustration, personality structure, attachment, and emotional regulation all contribute to the acquisition and development of self-control (Patterson & Newman, 1993). The comparative definition of frustration tolerance among theorists focuses on delayed gratification; However, a detailed explanation of Michelle's frustration tolerance can be summarized as a cognitive technique that can be used to control behavior in response to environmental stimuli.

The main component of frustration tolerance is the place of control. In general, people are often discouraged when they see that the environment controls or slows down the results, but those who slow down reactions tend to develop self-control (Mischel, 1986). Eisenberger et al. (1985) suggest that the effort needed to delay remuneration from an internal control center can be disappointing. People with low frustration tolerance tend to react impulsively to pollution so that it can be fulfilled immediately, achieve desired goals or avoid negative results. Therefore, people with low self-control (whether due to neurobiological trends or due to environmental and social influences) can obtain better impulse control through cognitive behavioral training, and small rewards with low self-control will gradually decrease more slowly. Barkley (1997) examines how leaders work to support this view, arguing that low frustration tolerance is related to impulsivity (as is ADHD), and cognitive and cognitive deficits influence sensitivity to increased learning of cognitive behavior. Cognitive behavioral disorders in dealing with frustration tolerance are very important for doctors who, when treating psychological disorders, should aim to slow down the satisfaction and tolerance of stress and emotions in various psychosocial dimensions to regulate themselves.

Personal structure and temperament also play a role in the development of self-control. Nigg et al. (2002) examined five personality dimensions related to impulsive and hyperactive ADHD symptoms and found a high correlation between ADHD and neuroticism and a low correlation with openness, kindness, extraversion, and conscientiousness. Paterson and Newman (1993) confirm this finding, but also find that extraversion is strongly associated with psychiatric disorders, suggesting that stable personality traits that persist into adulthood are associated with psychiatric disorders, including ADHD. In addition, Paterson and Newman argue that people who lack self-observation and self-reflection for personal gain and loss quickly respond to dissatisfaction and develop a lack of self-control because they cannot associate negative results with disinhibition. Nigg et al. also shows that impulsiveness is strongly associated with negative temperament and poor mood regulation. The implications of these results require a thorough assessment of the personality structure and temperature characteristics associated with impulse control deficits.

Gilliom et al. Examine the relationship between anger management and self-control. (2002) state that successful emotional regulation depends to a large extent on an individual's tendency to use coping strategies in response to external stimuli. Children who use adaptive techniques to perform difficult tasks, for example, can constantly reduce the intensity of their anger. Although there are individual differences in the techniques practiced by children, ranging from focusing on looking for attachment to parents, it has been found that using emotional regulation skills increases the effectiveness of self-control in general. This finding confirms that emotional regulation is related to self-control and shows that various strategies to overcome deficits can be effective in this area.

The effect of goal orientation on impulsivity also seems significant. When Chen and Vazsonyi (2011) compared young people with different future goals, they found that self-control was the highest among people with future prospects that were oriented and positive towards achieving goals. Barkley (1997) argues that the role of knowing the future implications for developing self-control is important for key leadership functions, with self-control enhanced by a continuous feedback cycle between self-regulating barrier language and achieving prize success. Similarly, Paterson and Newman (1993) argue that the ability to focus on the consequences facilitated by managerial planning and wise judgment triggers and enhances the ability to adapt to self-control. Alternatively, people with poorly modulated impulses cannot learn from negative events, think of the consequences, or develop predictive perspectives on the risk of impulsive behavior. Therefore, it is important for psychotherapists to recognize and examine an individual's focus on goals, insights, and regulatory skills to channel the potential for impulsivity and other psychiatric disorders.

INTERPERSONAL FACTORS THAT AFFECT SELF CONTROL

Humans and the environment play a major role when people learn, change and grow through their experience with the phenomenological world. "Social learning theory fits in with the explanation of human behavior in relation to the constant interaction between cognitive, behavioral and environmental determinants" (Bandura, 1977, p. Vii). This dynamic exchange can promote or inhibit self-control, depending on the neurological composition and reactions of individual life experiences. Barkley (1997) argues that the inherent functions of the executive and the maturation process basically create individual opportunities and tendencies for self-control, and that social norms and expectations shape the development of self-control over time. Vazsonyi and Huang (2010) suggest that self-control develops from positive experiences of socialization with caregivers, schools and community organizations, especially through modeling, assessing prosocial behavior and providing opportunities for learning discipline and delayed gratification. Data from long-term research supports the consensus that pulse patterns remain stable over time even without adaptive or therapeutic interventions.

Family of origin, especially parents and legal guardians, has a large impact on the acquisition and development of self-control (Berk, 2008; Bradley & Corwyn, 2007). The influence of parents on self-control starts early in life and has long lasting effects. The warmth and sensitivity of parents triggers the development of self-control at a young age by encouraging appropriate behavior (Berk, 2008). Parental warmth and commitment are important resources for developing self-control through participation, mutual respect, compliance, structured procedures, and controlled activities (Bradley & Corwyn, 2007). Parents and caregivers use various adaptive techniques to promote early childhood self-control, including sensitive responses to children's needs, encouraging linguistic expression, creating opportunities for independence and attention, and promoting compliance (Berk, 2008).

In this way, parental behavior and family dynamics can influence the development of self control. Strict parental control, excessive punishment, and abuse are associated with the lack of self-regulation and outward behavior observed in some psychological disorders (Bradley & Corwyn, 2007). Likewise, forced and impulsive parenting styles that use inadequate rules and disciplinary practices can reduce, jeopardize and endanger self-control in children (Bornovalova et al., 2013). Conflicting parenting styles among parents are not compatible with adaptive parenting skills that increase impulse control in children and often cause family conflict and psychological disorders, crime and lack of attention in children (Bornovalova et al., 2013). Children who do not learn to regulate the emotions and impulsive behavior of their families at home will often have social, academic and professional problems in the future (Fischer et al., 1990).

The quality of adult-parent-child relationships at home can have a negative impact on the development of self-control. Adult disputes can lead to immoral care practices and separation or divorce, and environmental instability often increases the likelihood of children developing problematic impulsive behavior (DeKlyen, 1996). Inadequate care units hinder the development of self-regulation skills through poor modeling, which can affect children's sense of security and adaptive socialization. Psychological disorders are common when parent-child relationships are affected by mental illness or other parental disabilities, such as lack of attachment, poor attachment, or lack of attention to children (DeKlyen, 1996). In such situations, doctors should consider working with parents and families of individual clients to overcome these deficiencies in the family unit.

Parental crime can also relate to psychological disorders in children. Antisocial parents are more likely to divorce their prosocial parents, suffer marital dysfunction, and use physical immunity as an immoral care method believed to be responsible for poor self-control in children. In addition, poor relationships between parents and children in families with antisocial parents predict destructive and antisocial behavior in children and adolescents (Bornovalova et al., 2013). Lahey et al. (1989) showed that maternal anti-social traits mediate impulsive behavior, as seen in ADHD and other psychiatric disorders, and McCarty and McMahon (2003) correlate with the education of a depressed mother with destructive pathology in adolescent boys. Children who grow up in such an environment can continue to display impulsive, anti-social and aggressive behavior in adulthood. Therefore, doctors in the environment must deal specifically with parental temperament, parenting practices, and stickiness issues.

Besides family of origin, social influence on the development of self-control comes from a variety of sources. While family and peers are still important influences, institutions, communities, media and socioeconomic conditions also moderate social learning at the individual level. Bronfenbrenner's (1994) environmental model best reflects the dynamics between these interpersonal factors and explains how an individual's social exchange with every aspect of society influences individual development. Community environments such as schools, places of worship and neighborhoods offer opportunities to acquire or hinder self-regulation skills through successful or unsuccessful peer interactions (Bradley & Corwyn, 2007). Involving peers, teachers, entrepreneurs, and leaders in the community in increasing compensation for individual efforts is a stable predictor of self-control in children and adolescents (Eisenberger et al., 1985). Mass media is also an important factor in achieving and maintaining self-control (Bandura, 1977). Bandura believes that modeling presentations in media programs can change the way people respond to perceived stimuli, change regulation, and emotional distress. Each of the above paradigms has strong implications that psychotherapists must take into account when developing self-regulation in vulnerable groups.

Socioeconomic Status (SES) is another important variable because research shows that low SES and poor living conditions contribute to impulsivity and psychological disorders (Johnson et al., 1999). Low parental income, education and professional status are prognostic factors for impulse control, mood and personality disorders and are associated with countless psychological disorders (Johnson et al., 1999). Poverty is associated with inadequate self-regulation skills (including emotional dysregulation and language deficits) in children of various ages (Bradley & Corwyn, 2007). Low socioeconomic conditions have a direct and indirect impact on the development of self-regulation, but interfere with people's adaptability and create conditions that are difficult for families to raise children (Baum et al., 1985). Low socio-economic environments hinder the development of adaptive coping strategies such as disturbances from stressful situations, which make people vulnerable to chronic stress (Gilliom et al., 2002). Doctors must consider the impact of all levels of society, SES, media and peers as relevant factors in the development of psychological disorders and other mental health problems.

AGGRESSION

Similar to self-control, understanding aggression is clear in any discussion about psychological disorders. Researchers tend to define aggression as the behavior they want to hurt, with the main components of poor self-control and anger disorders (Green, 1990). Although there are many types of aggression - instrumental, physical, verbal, and relational - it is the essence of dangerous behavior directed towards others (Berk, 2008). Bandura and Walters (1959) emphasize the component of damage and argue that aggression is synonymous with anti-social behavior which is dangerous and dangerous to others or property. Aggression can be seen as a physical act of real anger as a synonym of violence. Please note that our discussion of self-control deliberately precedes aggression to highlight the impulsivity inherent in aggression.

Aggression can also be seen as emotionally influenced by environmental pollution, especially in response to fainting. Bandura and Walters (1959) define frustration as "the emergence of conditions that prevent or delay the achievement of goal responses" (p. 89). Frustration is also described as an emotional state because abuse often precedes aggressive behavior (Baum et al., 1985). Impact regulation is associated with aggression - especially as an initial stage - where people with aggressive tendencies tend to react impulsively to emotional stress factors (Green, 1990). Therefore delayed gratification prevents destructive and aggressive complaints.

Very bad results can be caused by frustration, frustration throughout one's life. Loeber and Stouthamer Loeber (1998) document a high percentage of young people in nursing homes and schools who are abused because of abuse and abusive behavior. Adolescent offenders face many psychosocial problems in adulthood, including drug use, divorce, unemployment and legal difficulties (Loeber & Stouthamer-Loeber, 1998). Similarly, juvenile aggression was found to be significantly associated with depressive symptoms in adults (Diamantopoulos et al., 2011). In addition, poor tolerance of frustration can contribute to the rejection of friends if people behave impulsively and aggressively in social settings (Coie et al., 1992). These factors determine the direction of destructive and aggressive behavior, and it has been shown that aggression remains relatively stable over time (especially in highly disturbed people) (Loeber & Stouthamer-Loeber, 1998). These results indicate that psychotherapists must take into account the client's ability to tolerate dissatisfaction, delay gratification, and regulate emotions to reduce aggressive behavior.

It is important to recognize the character traits that underlie aggressive behavior. Potegal and Knutson (1994) suggest that irritability and emotional sensitivity are the main mediators of aggression. Green (1990) recognizes many additional factors that influence the development of aggression, including gender differences (men), cognitive development (low), and alcohol consumption (high). All of these variables need to be considered because they play an important role in weakening acquisitions and developing aggressive behavior.

INTRAERSONAL FACTORS THAT INFLUENCE AGGRESSION

Cognitive-behavioral framework prioritizes internal experiences rather than external stimuli. Therefore the development of aggression is understood by examining the role of individual interpretation or perception of an event and giving a negative meaning (Green, 1990). In fact, the perception of a person's situation is clearer than the situation itself; As a result, a stimulus only triggers aggression when it is seen by individuals as hostile or threatening (Zahn-Waxler et al., 1986).

In the cognitive-behavioral approach, internal dialogue leads to internal emotional experience, and subjective experience leads to the development and expression of aggression through various mechanisms. Ellis (2001) emphasizes the role of an irrational human belief system in the formation of an unhealthy neutral stimulation response that triggers negative reciprocal dynamics that can improve emotional symptoms at the diagnostic level. Beck also shows that people contribute to their own emotional discomfort by creating negative intellectual paradigms through automatic thought processes that trigger events (Alford & Beck, 1997). It is this distorted perception that makes one react aggressively to an impartial event that is triggered by a distorted, prejudiced, or personal understanding of the situation. Statements you make in the interests of survival can strengthen and reinforce negative assumptions and lead to violent behavior such as violence or harassment. To reduce the potential for aggression, counselors must help clients gain insight into their subjective psychological experiences by identifying irrational beliefs, distorted automatic responses, and negative self-statements.

Anger is an important interpersonal construction that is involved in the development of aggression. Negative influences, especially anger, tend to hide aggressive (though not violent) behavior which is usually based on perceived threats or injustices (Tangney et al., 1996). According to Berkovitz (1990), internal psychological processes combine anger with negative ideas, perceptions, Romanian tendencies and hostility. The methods by which people deal with anger and related knowledge are very different and have a direct impact on subsequent behavior (Tangney et al., 1996). For those who do not have adaptive coping strategies, for example, aggressive behavior can be a way out of unpleasant psychological and somatic experiences associated with anger (Berkowitz, 1990). According to Tangney et al. The level of insight into the emotional state and its meaning, which is inherent in the triggering event, correlates directly with the expression of aggressive behavior. Aggressive individuals tend to see their hostility, hatred, and irritability as self-defense, and are less concerned about the long-term effects of their aggressive actions on the recipient (Tangney et al., 1996). Developing adaptive coping skills to improve positive self management (especially in anger situations) and increase awareness and assess intracellular anger are important components of cognitive behavioral care for psychological disorders.

The ability to empathize, solve problems, and alleviate personal experiences with social interactions (including aggression) can be reversed, so that both deficits predispose to vulnerability to aggression (Zahn Waxler et al., 1986). In addition, low IQ, learning disabilities, and negative temperaments are found to be strongly associated with psychological disorders because they are related to cognitive deficits that change judgment, predict feelings of consistency, and impress others (Bandura & Walters, 1959)), aggression will most likely develop and increase when enhanced by positive results, namely achieving desired goals (Mischel, 1986). Expecting rewards for aggressive behavior tends to increase the likelihood of that behavior. Therefore, psychiatrists need to examine leadership, empathy and role reversal when assessing and treating mental and aggressive disorders.

The psychological construction of intentionality as an integral part of aggression must also be overcome. Baum et al. (1985) explain that society does not deviate from all forms of aggression, even though it intends to damage the basis of each aggression. For example, athletes, caring people and authoritarian people regularly engage in aggressive behavior that is acceptable when facing problems and forces children to obey them (for example, by removing toys) or making arrests. Intention is also a broad term - whether the behavior is fully implemented, the intention to violate the action is considered aggressive. For example, a failed attempt is considered as aggressive as what has been done.

The Social Information Processing Model (SIP) examines cognitive coding sequences, interpretations, and reactions in the development of aggressive behavior. Zahn-Waxler et al. (1986) argue that certain aggressive outcomes - such as anger, hostility towards others, or hyperrealism towards stimuli - result from distortions in this information processing sequence. The doctor must identify and correct this disorder (e.g. miscoding and misinterpretation) to stop the development and development of aggressive impulses.

INTERPERSONAL FACTORS THAT INFLUENCE AGGRESSION

As suggested by Arsenio and Lémeris (2010), no source can be unilaterally responsible for aggression. Conversely, aggression can be triggered by the interaction of complementary psychological, ecological, and social factors. While destructive appeals, including aggression, are related to some extent, social learning theory argues that aggression is mediated through empirical experience rather than individual knowledge (Berk, 2008) and that the greatest impact on the development of aggression is not biologically motivated. and efforts to learn from external sources (Bandura, 1977). Impersonation and reinforcement are basic principles that encourage social learning, and imitation involves direct observation and modeling of environmental stimuli, whereas imitation involves promotion or payment of behavior through gifts or punishment. People learn by experiencing, observing and dealing with their environment and exposing themselves to family, community, social economy and the media as a source of learning and aggression.

Individual families seem to have the greatest influence on learned behavior. Most of the results of the study show a strong relationship between family experience and aggressive behavior (Shaver & Mikulincer, 2011). Peters et al. (1992) stated that living together with antisocial fathers, depressed mothers or alcoholic parents contributed to the development of violent or abusive behavior. Likewise, it was found that parents' negative perceptions about their home family mediated the development of aggression in their children (DeKlyen, 1996). The current style of care is shaped by the care style of previous generations, and immoral care practices lead to aggression and suffering in children, mainly due to lack of warmth and rejection from the mother. Therefore, doctors must review multi-generational family systems to determine whether these key factors of aggression can occur. Inadequate parent-child interaction is a well-documented determinant of children's aggression (Bornalova et al., 2013): "Parental violence can be a model of aggression and contribute to a forced parent-child conflict style" (Bradley) & Corwyn , 2007, Pages. 1391). Forced care, which requires an aggressive reaction in children, can cause spontaneous physical punishment, neglect, rejection, abuse, excessive anger, and rejection of love and care (Lefkowitz et al., 1977). Doctors must review these factors because they significantly influence the development of aggression and psychological disorders in children.

The promotion of youth extends beyond the family to the local and larger community. Such an environment acts as a resource to develop aggressive tendencies, either through direct contact or through media surveillance (Baum et al., 1985). An environment full of violence, crime or harassment offers opportunities for people who are exposed to aggressive prejudice. For example, there is a well-documented significant relationship between aggression and harsh environments, such as low-income housing and overcrowded child care centers (Peters et al., 1992). In addition, life in low-income urban communities is usually associated with high stress and additional deviant effects that promote aggression (Gilliom et al., 2002). Loeber and Stouthamer-Loeber (1998) show that aggression tends to increase and decrease due to the presence or absence of other aggressive colleagues. Some researchers even suggest that environmental propaganda, as seen in crime, serves as a protection against the pressures of the urban environment (Baum et al., 1985), thus encouraging the development of aggression. Although these factors are beyond the physician's control, psychotherapists need to be sensitive to the patient's environment to recognize and respond to their effects on aggressive tendencies.

Mass communication socialization also promotes the development of aggression, specifically by providing impressive reproducible materials (Lefkowitz et al., 1977) and by expressing public signals about aggressive behavior such as acceptance, retaliation and attachment to aggression also justification for violence (Green, 1990). Media images appear to have a long-term impact on the development of aggression and often promote aggression by reducing sensitivity to violence. Baum et al. (1985) suggested that media violence causes aggressive behavior in boys, which is reflected in puberty and adulthood. In addition, media image content in the socialization process seems important as a model for violence (through graphical representation of weapons, crime and fighting). Aggression manifests itself in boys, whereas the absence of female aggressors weakens the influence of the media on girls (Lefkowitz et al 1977). According to Burke (2008), the influence of the media on aggression is widespread from time to time due to the influence of their habits. Children become more aggressive because they do not associate long-term effects with images with crude characters (for example in animated films or video games). Although consultants cannot limit the influence of the media on the development of aggression, doctors can actively focus on how individuals interact and feel their ecological and psychosocial influences in order to develop strategies to overcome or reduce these negative influences.

Although many psychological and developmental factors influence acquisition, self-control, and aggression, the specific pattern of these influences causes various psychiatric disorders.

ATTENTION DEFICIT HYPERACTIVITY DISORDER (ADHD)

The main symptoms of ADHD are excessive impulsivity and lack of attention to development. ADHD is diagnosed as a negligent or impulsive type of hyperactivity, with diagnostic criteria aimed at diverting or inability to maintain self-controlled behavior (American Psychiatric Association [APA], 2013). Self-control is very important for the diagnosis of ADHD. While aggression is not an important symptom of this disorder, aggressive outbreaks often accompany the main symptoms, especially in young children. People with ADHD show great variability in their ability to regulate attention and control impulses in different situations (Barkley, 1997). For example, children, teenagers, or adults with ADHD may play video games for a long time, but may have difficulty staying at school or at work. Cognitive deficits are often the cause of self-control problems that occur in many people with ADHD, and environmental factors (such as forced parent-child interaction) also contribute to the development of psychological disorders (Nigg et al., 1998).

OPPOSITIONAL DISRUPTIVE DISORDER, ODD

The main symptoms of oppositional disruptive disorder (ODD) are anger, irritability, revenge and challenging behavior (APA, 2013). These behaviors are based on impulsivity, aggression, and especially verbal aggression. Limited self control in ODD is seen as a function where emotions cannot be effectively managed, which often causes excessive anger and challenges. With the exception of the plague, people with ODD do not act violently or violate the rights of others. Conversely, verbal or covert aggression is more typical, e.g. B .: Angry behavior or deliberate outburst of anger. In addition, ODD is often associated with ADHD, highlighting the main aspects of impulsivity as symptoms of both disorders resulting from difficulties that resist destructive impulses. As with ADHD, AR3 symptoms are often associated with cognitive deficits of parents and unintentional interactions (Lahey et al., 1989).

CONDUCT DISORDER, CD

Conduct disorders (CDs) are usually open attacks, including personal injury, theft or property damage (APA, 2013). Ignoring social norms and violating other people's personal rights are the defining features of CD (APA, 2013). While impulsivity can increase CD, violent physical aggression is the dominant feature of this disorder. Research shows that parental personality and parenting style are strong predictors of CD (Lahey et al., 1989). Similarly, CD is an important predictor of antisocial personality disorder in adults (APA, 2013), and those with behavioral disorders often have a poor prognosis and poor treatment outcomes. Therefore environmental actions (formal or legal) may be needed.

TIC DISORDER

Movement or automatic vocalization determines all tic disorders, including Tourette's, the worst of the four tic disorders (APA, 2013). The symptoms of flea disorders are exacerbated by stress, and the environment and psychosocial stimuli provide a destructive impulse that underlies this diagnosis. Impaired self control is at the heart of the tic's impulsive nature, and the strength of the impulse and lack of awareness of physical and cognitive traps influences the extent to which symptoms are expressed.

INTERMITTENT EXPLOSIVE DISORDER, IED

Intermittent Explosive Disorder (IED) is characterized by impulsivity and aggression. Symptoms include rare but significant personal outbreaks or property damage that is not proportionate to the cause of the beating (APA, 2013). Aside from violence, people with IEDs are usually calm and regret their actions after the plague. Although physically violent and aggressive, the devastating consequences are the result of the inability to regulate self-regulation. In certain situations, people with IEDs can be exposed to extreme pressures that exceed the expected limit, overcome coping skills, and hinder them. General characteristics are social information, knowledge, and environmental factors (such as stress).

MOOD DISORDER

Some mood disorders include symptoms of irritability and can be characterized by persistence and disruptive behavior due to irritability. Symptoms of DMDD in some communities with IED include a combination of low self-control and physical or verbal aggression (APA, 2013). They express themselves in explosions, flashes of inspiration and irritated moods that continue between episodes. Cognitive deficits that support reduced tolerance of impotence and impaired anger modulation associated with DMDD. Because this diagnosis is aimed at children and adolescents (especially to prevent over diagnosis of bipolar disorder in children), people with DMDD are very vulnerable to social and environmental impacts on the needs of the disorder, including family dynamics and lack of parental self-control. and increased aggression. Peer ratios often worsen the severity of symptoms (Pope & Bierman, 1999).

People with bipolar disorder can also have impulsive and aggressive nature. Psychological disorders associated with self-disorders often characterize symptoms of mania in particular. This is illustrated by quick / free solutions and hasty decisions, which may include excessive hypersexuality and psychomotor arousal caused by hostility and anger caused by mood swings. intense and potentially dangerous for you or others (APA, 2013). Although genetic factors are often associated with bipolar disorder, environmental factors, and psychosocial risks, symptoms can be exacerbated and affect people's reactions to situational triggers. For example, defects in cognitive structures, which often form the basis for poor impulse control and cognitive prejudice against aggressive reactions, tend to interact with biological factors as causes of devastating symptoms and behavior. Because the symptoms of bipolar disorder are often attempts at suicide and this suicide coupled with a diagnosis of bipolar disorder, it is important for doctors to specifically treat the impulsive and aggressive aspects of bipolar disorder. . Disturbance. .

PERSONALITY DISORDER

The two most common personality disorders are associated with unregulated, anti-social and emergent personality disorders. Impulsiveness is an important symptom of disorder and aggression is an important symptom of an anti-social personality disorder (APA, 2013). Anti-social people tend to be the rights of others and can often be angry and impulsive when they aggressively try to meet their own needs. Cognitive structures do not have a clear impact on the behavior of people with PSA, because they usually don't do it for others. The socioeconomic deficit of parents is a strong predictor of PSA, so these factors need to be assessed. Lack of empathy and arrogance can lead to violence and other criminal behavior and often require legal placement and intervention (as a corrective measure).

Personality disorders are characterized by significant impulse problems associated with severe emotional dysregulation (APA, 2013). This is a major psychosocial disorder with fear of death and problems between them. Incorrect understanding of environmental triggers often leads to feelings of hopelessness, which result in target behavior being slightly modulated and intense to reduce feelings of abandonment and rejection. Patterns of instability and parental dysfunction in close romantic relationships are usually associated with illness, and so many other family members may or may not be involved.

OTHER DISORDERS WITH DESTRUCTIVE FUNCTIONS

Neurocognitive disorders, intellectual disorders, and the autism spectrum require inclusion, because people with this disorder often have aspects of self-control and aggression. People with delirium, neurocognitive disorders (previously dementia in the fourth edition of the Handbook on Statistics for Diagnostic and Psychiatric Disorders) and autism spectrum disorders can show aggression to various levels with strong symptoms (APA, 2013). Examples of aggression can be verbal reasons that can be accessed by the public or shop. The pathogenesis of this disease can vary, but self-control requires impaired cognitive structure, which is often related to the severity of the outbreak. Because people with this disease often live with family members or in a supportive environment, considering environmental factors is very important.

This chapter discusses the main psychological and developmental factors associated with psychological disorders. The basic terms self-control (impulse control) and aggression form the basis for destructive behavior and behavior. While various theoretical perspectives can help to understand these factors, cognitive approaches to behavior are most commonly used to conceptualize the psychopathology underlying psychiatric disorders. Many ecological, cognitive, and social factors have been shown to influence the acquisition, development, and course of self-control and aggression, particularly instability in the family, disruption in childcare, cruel childcare practices, experiences of violence and socio-economic deficits. Antisocial relationships of affiliation, different reinforcements and rewards, cognitive impairment, and deficiencies in information processing. Individual differences in prejudice and stimulus reactions are clear and compel doctors to rethink these factors on a case-by-case basis. In addition, for related reasons, other related factors (e.g. gender and cultural determinants) are not discussed in this chapter. Physicians are encouraged to pursue a broad perspective to understand the psychological and developmental effects of lack of self-control and aggression, and use this broad understanding to develop holistic approaches to treating the symptoms of psychiatric disorders.

CHAPTER FOUR
EPIDEMIOLOGY OF PSYCHOLOGICAL DISORDERS

Psychological disorders can inherently affect how people, families, communities and society function. For example, Copeland et al. (2011) found in the Big Smoky Mountain study that men were more likely to be diagnosed with psychiatric disorders. This difference is caused by gender differences in mental stress. This violation is also related to large monetary costs. Pelham et al. (2007) estimated that the average annual cost of care for children with Attention Deficit Hyperactivity Disorder (ADHD) was $ 2636, $ 2,900 for education, and $ 7,044 for all crimes and crimes per child with ADHD per year. De Graaf et al. (2008) found that adults in 10 countries lost an average of 22.1 years more days. High price and high impact. This chapter discusses the epidemiology and course of these diseases to better understand the extent of the effects of these diseases and their impact on people throughout their lives.

SUPREMACY

As explained in this chapter, psychological disorders almost always begin in childhood. However, before we look at the prevalence of childhood psychiatric disorders, we need to be aware of the limitations of this field of research, because assessing the epidemiology of child psychiatry poses certain challenges. One challenge is the lack of sufficiently sensitive and concrete steps. Serious psychological disorders, such as those needed in epidemiological studies, are common in adults and cannot understand the developmental changes associated with these disorders in young people (Costello et al., 2005).

Costello et al. (2005) also found that the use of DLA (Disabled Living Age) would be more appropriate to measure the severity of children's psychiatric problems. But in practice, DLA is rarely counted and reported. It is only in the last 15 years that psychiatric problems in children are measured in epidemiological studies (Costello et al., 2005). However, the following information must be considered reasonable given the limitations mentioned above.

DHF that stands out is ADHD. In a sample of the youth community, Roberts et al. (2007) found a 12-month prevalence of ADHD of 2.06%. Merikangas et al. (2010) found a 12-month ADHD incidence higher in children aged 8-15 years using data from the 2001-2004 National Health and Nutrition Examination Survey, which was 7.8%. These differences can reflect differences between age groups. Willcutt (2012) conducted a meta-analysis and estimated the combined prevalence in children and adolescents by 5.9%. Each of these ranks shows a significant proportion of young people with regulatory concerns and behavioral problems.

In any case, ADHD is lopsidedly appropriated crosswise over populace socioeconomics. Barkley (2003) refers to past research and found that ADHD among African-Americans is by all accounts expanding. In any case, he clarified that this rate can be misdirecting on the grounds that it is just founded on the instructor's conduct report. He additionally noticed that when controlling for comorbid conditions, financial status (SES) didn't assume a significant job in the spread of ADHD (Barkley, 2003). Utilizing later information, Schieve et al. (2012) utilized the 2006-2010 National Wellbeing Meeting Review to analyze the statistic information of kids with ADHD. More than 66% of ADHD respondents state they are male. Most of individuals with ADHD distinguish themselves as white Hispanic individuals, and their moms are bound to get an advanced education than optional school. Russell et al. (2013) found from the English Thousand years Companion Concentrate that youngsters with ADHD were bound to be male, have lower intellectual capacities, have a more youthful gestational age and more youthful moms. The predominance of ADHD in men proceeds into adulthood. Cumyn et al. (2009) found altogether a bigger number of men than ladies with ADHD even in adulthood. Along these lines, the seriousness of the sickness is by all accounts dependent on specific populaces.

Restriction evaluation (ODD) is altogether different. Boylan et al. (2007) directed a meta-examination of the commonness of DRR in youngsters. Coefficients go from 1.8% to 15.4%, in spite of the fact that it isn't resolved whether the gauge is for a year or the lifetime commonness (Boylan et al., 2007). Roberts et al. (2007) found a year conveyance of 2.77% in the network test. Merikangas et al. (2010), in light of NHANES information, had comparative outcomes and a year predominance of 2.1% among youngsters matured 8 to 15 years. Nock et al. (2007) found a lifetime commonness of 10.2%. This region of prevalence estimation may reflect contrasts in the strategies used to compute pervasiveness gauges (for example instructor parent overviews, year life length conveyance) and contrasts in estimating instruments. Albeit ODD has been accounted for to be increasingly regular in men (Quy and Stringaris, 2012), enormous scale epidemiological information show that there are no critical sexual orientation contrasts (Nock et al., 2007). Individuals with ODD are bound to have lower SES foundations and experience constrained parenthood (Quy and Stringaris, 2012).

Comparative levels can likewise be found in individuals with conduct issue (CD). Nock et al. (2006), in light of Replication of the National Komorbitas Replication, recorded a lifetime CD pervasiveness of 9.5%. In an example of immature networks, Roberts et al. (2007) found a year pervasiveness of 3.32%. The plausibility of being determined to have a Cd during life is related with "youthful age, men, low training, separation or separation, living arrangement in the western US and city home" (Nock et al., 2006, p. 5).

There are blended outcomes on whether there are sexual orientation contrasts in ODD or CD. Roberts et al. (2007) found that men experiencing ODD or CD were essentially more successive than ladies, albeit statistic information identified with ODD was considered, Nock et al. (2007) found no noteworthy contrasts among people. Maughan et al. (2004), who examined ODD and CD in the Assembled Realm, found that CD were fundamentally more typical in young men than young ladies, and recurrence demonstrated a direct pattern with a higher rate with age in both genders after some time. . ODD is additionally more typical in young men than young ladies (Maughan et al., 2004). These blended discoveries require further examination.

There is in like manner a passing quality to ODD. For ODD, the center time of starting is assessed to be 12.0 (Nock et al., 2007). Those in the most negligible age packs were viewed as on a very basic level less slanted to have ODD or Plate than those in focus immaturity or young person years (Roberts et al., 2007). Likewise, those with ODD or Minimal plate were basically progressively disinclined to have hitched watchmen (Roberts et al., 2007).

The inescapability of two other psychological issue, Tourette's issue and IED, has been evaluated moreover. The Living spaces for Ailment Control and Abhorrence checks that three for each 1,000 youngsters developed 6–17 have a parent report a lifetime finish of Tourette's issue. Among those with examined Tourette's issue, youngsters predominated young women by three to one, and those dissected were twice as inclined to be progressively settled, rather than increasingly energetic, teenagers (Territories for Disorder Control and Expectation, 2009). When investigating young people as an element of the National Comorbidity Survey Replication, McLaughlin et al. (2012) found a lifetime normality of IED of 5.3%, and equivalent results were found with adults (Kessler et al., 2006). The typical number of ambushes through the range of a month was 11.8 (Kessler et al., 2006).

With the dispersion of the fifth arrival of the Characteristic and Indicative and Factual Manual of Psychological Issue (DSM-5), another Psychological issue, hazardous perspective dysregulation issue was exhibited. This issue depicts kids with extraordinary energetic and social disturbance and nonepisodic irritability. The investigation is obliged for this issue, anyway normality can be extrapolated from existing instructive files. Copeland et al. (2013) utilized existing diagrams and pulled out those with signs dependable with DMDD. Of the three examinations utilized, paces of DMDD went from 0.8% (Contemplating Children in the System study) to 3.3% (Duke Preschool Apprehension Study). Among those with symptoms of DMDD, there were generally progressively vital incapacitations in parental and educator relations, more school suspensions, increasingly imperative assistance use both in mental prosperity and therapeutic settings, increasingly huge degrees of poverty, and more prominent likelihood of being raised in a single parent family and having watchmen with low degrees of preparing (Copeland et al., 2013). Since DMDD has been added to the DSM, additional examination will likely be coordinated later on.

Psychological disorder can in like manner appear as a bit of various issue. Direct exacerbation—especially fractiousness, antagonistic vibe, and wrath—is an inside segment of bipolar disorder, anyway these signs habitually spread with comorbid disperses, for instance, ODD and ADHD (Hammen and Rudolph, 2003). Youths with substance awkwardness go issue have been noted to show psychological disorder, for instance, self-harm, decreased necessity for rest (Klinger et al., 2003), fits, tension, and assurance (Brereton et al., 2006). According to extents of psychological disorder, kids with concoction unevenness run issue fall in the 66th percentile diverged from those with academic powerlessness (Brereton et al., 2006).

Patients with personality disorder, especially peripheral personality disorder (BPD) and saved personality disorder (ASPD), normally display psychological disorder as a significant part of the disarray. The regularity of BPD is evaluated to be 1.4% of the US masses and ASPD 0.6% (Lenzenweger et al., 2007). When investigated on a people level, there is an example exhibiting progressively important likelihood of folks resolved to have ASPD (Lenzenweger et al., 2007), and about 75% of those resolved to have BPD are females (American Mental Alliance [APA], 2013). Self-mutilation is a logical part of

BPD, with such direct occurring in up to 80% of those dissected, and individuals with BPD show an extended threat of private accessory brutality (as alluded to in Sansone and Sansone, 2012).

Psychological disorder can reach out over an individual's future. Among those resolved to have dementia, 45.1% have been found to have at any rate one psychological disorder symptom, on a very basic level more than those resolved to have smooth mental obstruction (Chan et al., 2005). Psychological disorder should be considered over the future.

COMORBID CONDITIONS

Exactly as expected, DBDs routinely don't occur in division. Research has been driven on youth with summarized direct issues. Polier et al. (2012) considered adolescents with parent-recognized general lead or masking issues. In this system test, 10.6% were found to have a sort of lead issue, with 3.7% having a covering camouflaging issue. This degree of spread was not actually in a relationship clinical model, which utilized dynamically express demonstrative criteria and earnestness rules, in which 25.8% had comorbid externalizing and camouflaging jumbles. Inside the system and clinical models there was increasingly vital reality of social issues for those with direct and masking issues when appeared differently in relation to those simply having conduct issues (Polier et al., 2012). As such camouflaging and externalizing jumbles every now and again co-occur and may have near etiologies.

Individuals with ADHD are more plausible than those without ADHD to have learning issue. A critical portion (41.3%) of youngsters with ADHD, in perspective on the

National Prosperity Meeting Audit, also had a comorbid learning issue (Schieve et al., 2012). Larsson et al. (2012) found in a general sense extended peril of learning issue among those with ADHD. Learning issue may include to patients conveying in the school and expert settings, as those with unfamiliar learning failures as often as possible become bewildered, controlling the signs of their comorbid psychological disorder.

There is moreover extended peril of strain and wretchedness among those with ADHD. Larsson et al. (2012) discovered through and through higher risk of strain and wretchedness among those with ADHD. Likewise, among adults with ADHD, appeared differently in relation to those without, there were out and out higher paces of ADHD-express dread, social dread, alert issue, and noteworthy difficult issue (Cumyn et al., 2009). These comorbid issue also can fuel the current psychological disorder and subsequently should be studied while investigating an individual and their lead presentation.

Furthermore, ADHD may co-occur with a developmental issue. Larsson et al. (2012) found extended peril of substance irregularity go issue among kids with ADHD. Those with the two issue may show an additional substance sway in the reality of the symptoms. Gadow et al. (2006) looked occupation of ADHD among youths with mental irregularity go issue and found that those with the two issue had progressively unmistakable reality of indications and will undoubtedly be on remedies.

There is furthermore extended peril for co-occasion of psychological disorder. Larsson et al. (2012) found extended peril for direct issue and Tourette's issue. Basically higher paces of past (anyway not present) clinically tremendous signs of direct issue and pulled back personality disorder similarly existed among adults (Cumyn et al., 2009). Extended peril of substance use moreover appears to occur among adults with ADHD. Van Emmerik-van Oortmerssen et al. (2012) coordinated a met examination on the inescapability of ADHD in substance abuse patients and found that 23.1% of patients in the substance abuse bundle had comorbid ADHD. Potential direct irritation found in those with substance abuse gives thusly may be the presence of comorbid ADHD. As a rule, inferable from the high paces of comorbid conditions with ADHD, one should characteristically think about the extent of potential decisions while concerning a person's lead profile.

There is an essentially higher danger of comorbid ODD with different issue, explicitly state of mind issue, nervousness issue, motivation control issue, or substance misuse issue. It ought to be noticed that solitary 42.5% of patients with ODD keep on creating CD and 25% experience the ill effects of ADHD comorbidity (Nock et al., 2007). The frequency of comorbid sadness with ODD is somewhere in the range of 2.4% and 45.4% and practically all examinations show an essentially more elevated level of discouragement contrasted with youths without ORD. The pervasiveness of comorbid tension issue ranges from 7.1% to 55.3% with the chances proportion expanding correspondingly contrasted with those without ODD (Boylan et al., 2007).

Research has likewise been directed on teenagers with more than one psychological disorder. Among those influenced by CD, subsequent to representing age and different irregularities, there was a noteworthy increment in the paces of ADHD comorbidity in young men and young ladies and gloom in young men. Comparative outcomes have been found in patients with ODD and there is likewise an expanded danger of comorbid tension (Maughan et al., 2004). With such high coefficients, particularly those identified with ADHD, the conspicuous yet unanswered inquiry is whether these anomalies speak to various issue or whether the cover is enormous to such an extent that the side effects speak to a similar range of variations from the norm. This thought has indicative ramifications, and concentrates on the predominance and course of psychological disorder must think about this chance.

Other than ADHD, ODD and other DBD additionally have significant levels of comorbid conditions. Individuals with Touret's issue have a high pace of comorbidity with ADHD, other social or conduct issue, uneasiness issue, gloom or formative postponements (Habitats for Infection Control and Counteractive action, 2009). It has been discovered that youths with IED are analyzed fundamentally more frequently than the all inclusive community with fears, alarm issue, nervousness issue with detachment or misuse or illicit drug use. While considering patients with extreme issue contrasted with patients with less IED scenes, the probability of medication misuse or chronic drug use is essentially higher (McLauglin et al., 2012).

Individuals with bipolar disorder have high paces of comorbid psychological disorder, for example, ADHD (34.7% of patients with bipolar disorder), ADHD (24.3%), other undefined psychological disorder (18.1%) and CD. (4.2%)%; Youngstrom et al., 2005). Accordingly, these disarranges will in general be very comorbid with one another.

The job of hereditary covers between scatters is another field of research. Faraone et al. (2012) directed a meta-examination of ADHD and Bipolar I likelihood and found a huge increment in ADHD chance in individuals with hereditary hazard for Bipolar I (chance proportion = 2.6), including heredity, kin, and guardians. There is additionally an expanded danger of Bipolar I in individuals with an expanded hereditary hazard for ADHD. These outcomes show that you don't must have family members with specific issue, and even the hereditary danger of those disarranges can expand the opportunity of creating different issue.

COURSE OF PSYCHOLOGICAL DISORDER

A few arbitrary pathways can prompt the advancement of explicit DBD over the whole age. Understanding the bearing of creating DBD gives data about treatment alternatives and aides in the improvement of early intercession and aversion programs. People can differ in the beginning and course of DBD (Farris et al., 2011) and can run from minor side effects from one issue to complex manifestations from a few issue. As a result of its numerous practices, the field of externalizing conduct is only one measurement, from aloofness to rash/hyperactive to battling physical animosity.

ADHD
CHILDREN AND ADOLESCENT

Advances in the improvement of social issue portray ADHD. By and large, ADHD indications regularly happen in preschool years, as a rule between the ages of 3 and 4 (Wilens and Spencer, 2010), albeit a few side effects have been recently detailed. Hyperactive engine conduct, for example, exorbitant exercise during rest, has been seen to happen between ages 1 and 1.5 years (Loeber et al., 2000). Other hyperactive hasty engine practices saw in youngsters matured 3 to 5 years incorporate exorbitant climbing, over the top running inside, trouble playing smoothly, poor resistance for disappointment and deficiencies in versatile conduct (Vierhile et al., 2009). At home and at school, these youngsters are seen by more established grown-ups as being progressively indiscreet, forceful and requesting and have more unfortunate social aptitudes (DeWolfe et al., 2000; Egger and Angold, 2006). On the off chance that extreme hyperactive engine conduct and careless conduct have been seen in preschool kids for over one year, these youngsters are probably going to be determined to have ADHD in youth and immaturity (Reef et al., 2011).

From elementary school age 6 to 12, extra ADHD conduct starts to create. Animosity issues can happen in younger students with ADHD (Hinshaw, 2002). ADHD Newborn children have additionally been distinguished as antecedents for social issues in youthfulness and early adulthood (Mannuzza et al., 2004; Mordre et al., 2011). In youth (around 12 years), issues of official working identified with ADHD start to altogether impact self-guideline (Barkley et al., 2001) and versatile capacity (Barkley et al., 1996). Therefore, kids with ADHD may have extra issues with social inability and enthusiastic prosperity (Wehmeier et al., 2010). While interfacing with friends, youngsters and youths with ADHD may experience issues teaming up, turning, and trading, or might be narrow minded, hasty, or unfriendly. Thus, youngsters with ADHD are bound to be dismissed by their friends (Becker et al., 2012; Hoza, 2007). Families with kids with ADHD experience escalated struggle among youngsters and guardians, which might be brought about by the kid's conduct, dismissal for rules or correspondence troubles (Wehmeier et al., 2010). Accordingly, a youngster with ADHD can endure noteworthy enthusiastic pressure (Escobar et al., 2005, for example, B. Gloom (Daviss et al., 2009) and confidence (Klimkeit et al., 2006), which can thusly causing pressure further improves the probability of psychological disorder.

Most of children with ADHD will in general keep on experiencing this issue in youthfulness (Biederman et al., 2000). As youngsters with ADHD create in teenagers, the seriousness of their side effects can diminish. Hyperactive incautious conduct specifically shows the most huge lessening; Be that as it may, careless conduct is the most difficult and hazardous conduct in young people (Biederman et al., 2000; Loeber et al., 2000). Numerous components appear to add to the industriousness of ADHD from youth to youthfulness, remembering the degree of hyperactive rash conduct for adolescence, which prompts issues, resistance conduct, antagonistic vibe and parent-kid strife (Barkley, 2003; Taylor et al. , 1996)), these components are likewise significant indicators of comorbid resistance and social issue in youths with youth ADHD (Hart et al., 1995; Mannuzza et al., 2004; Taylor et al., 1996; Yoshimasu et al., 2012). The nearness of hyperactivity, absence of consideration and absence of motivation control have been demonstrated to be emphatically associated with future standoffish conduct (Herpertz et al., 2001; Hinshaw et al., 1993; Holmes et al., 2001; Mandel, 1997). Kids with ADHD with overwhelmingly hyperactive rash side effects are bound to develop CD and ODD later in adulthood and keep up their solitary conduct than kids with particularly careless side effects (Caspi et al., 1995; Dykman and Acherman, 1993; Holmes, 2001). In kids matured 25 years, a conclusion of ADHD in adolescence is related with an expanded plausibility of tenacious and expanded psychosocial and psychological disorder, including bipolar disorder, conduct issue (Mannuzza et al., 2004) and serious despondency (Biederman et al. , 2009). .).

ADULTS

The adult abatement pace of ADHD was seen to arrive at 60%, with a noteworthy decrease in the indicative subcategory (Biederman et al., 2000). Clinically, grown-ups who have been determined to have ADHD can be incautious, careless and restless, like kids and teenagers who have been determined to have something very similar (Biederman et al., 2000, 2009), yet for some grown-ups, seriousness hyperactivity can be altogether diminished in adolescence, in spite of the fact that side effects of negligence and impulsivity endure (Koumoula, 2012). ADHD side effects in adulthood can significantly affect the expert, monetary, social and passionate prosperity of grown-ups with ADHD, including lower money related assets, lower levels of instruction, more unfortunate work execution, and more noteworthy social prohibition (Brod et al, 2012). ADHD manifestations as a rule decline in adulthood (Jacobs et al., 2007; Kessler et al., 2005).

OPPOSITE AND CONDUCT DISORDER
CHILDREN AND ADOLESCENT

All through life, the course of ODD and CD is very reliable and unsurprising, regardless of the particular geology of conduct change with improvement (Hinshaw and Lee, 2003). Showdown and poise blasts in preschool kids go before physical hostility in youth and end and robbery, lying, demolition of property and conceivable rape in pre-adulthood. Many recommend a relationship among ODD and CD, with ODD being an antecedent to CD advancement (Burke et al., 2010; Loeber et al., 2000), despite the fact that the two sicknesses stay isolated (Rowe et al., 2010) and can be analyzed simultaneously . For instance, the analysis of RR in young people matured 4 to 6 years is prescient Disc with early beginning in 79% of cases (Burke et al., 2010), and young men with low degrees of restriction CD conduct are in the longitudinal gathering. not found. DBD examination (Loeber et al., 2000). In any event, while controlling for ADHD and financial components, young men with ODD are at expanded danger of being determined to have Disc sometime down the road (Loeber et al., 2000). Be that as it may, not all kids with ODD have CD (Burke et al., 2010; Rowe et al., 2010).

Like ADHD, indications of ODD and CD happen in kids at a youthful age and in preschool. One of the main side effects is the dismissal for rules, which are normal for ODD and CD (Petitclerc et al., 2009). It might be hard for 3-year-old youngsters to recognize improper formative conduct from tests to control and control conduct. Eger and Heavenly attendant (2006) propose discontinuous conditions to characterize DSM criteria for preschool conduct contrasts that frequently happen from social issues: grown-up outrage misfortune (a few times each day), grown-up debates (two times per week), dynamic grown-ups characterize (five times each day), purposely upsetting others (five times each week), charging others (when a week) and acting furious and irate (when daily; Egger and Angold, 2006; Wakschlag et al., 2012). As indicated by Egger and Angold (2006), kids who surpass this edge worth may have conduct issues that are as per ODD.

ODD and CD related conduct additionally increments. The assessed normal age for event of ODD side effects is 6 years and 9 years for CD (Hinshaw and Lee, 2003). Kids matured 4 to 6 years with ODD (yet without Cd) can show an abatement in side effects of ODD following 6 to 7 years, however they can in any case show an elevated level of useful harm (Burke et al., 2010). In a longitudinal investigation of DBD in young men, Loeber et al. (2000) express that paying little respect to whether side effects show up in adolescence (7 to 9 years) or later in youth (10 to 12 years), social issues are generally brought about by resistance conduct and afterward cause pitilessness to creatures at home . lying, consuming, taking robbery and afterward battling (Loeber et al., 2000). Physical battle predicts CD inclusion more than different side effects (Loeber et al., 1995). Visit conduct with less genuine outcomes, for example, visit swearing and fleeing from home, regularly saw in youth (Loeber et al., 2000). In progressively extreme instances of teenagers with CDs and noteworthy dark and non-enthusiastic highlights, indications will in general start in youth (Frick, 2012). The more youthful the youngster is toward the start of his conduct, the quicker his conduct creates from the less extreme to the most genuine (Loeber et al., 1992; McMahon et al., 2010). The previous the conduct, the more troublesome and bizarre later solitary conduct, for example, theft, assault, burglary and interruption (Loeber et al., 2000).

ADULTS

Reserved conduct (ASBs) for the most part alludes to the conduct of teenagers or youthful grown-ups who have PPE attributes however don't meet the full prerequisites for PPE conclusion (e.g., no past Disc analysis; Goldstein et al., 2012). Individuals who create ASB later in youthfulness will in general have less intellectual shortfalls, higher intelligence level scores, better scholastic execution, and better passionate self-guideline aptitudes (Frick, 2012; Moffitt and Caspi, 2001); Walters and Knight, 2010).

In spite of the fact that ASB youths additionally will in general be related with insidious friends, young people with ASB episodes may later have more elevated levels of parental contribution and control, lower levels of misuse and misuse, fundamental fixings, and higher SES (Frick, 2012; Moffitt and Caspi, 2001). For them, the beginning of ASB can be related with the beginning of pubescence (Moffitt and Caspi, 2001). The previous manifestations and infringement happen, the almost certain the individual will keep on disregarding their conduct (Walters and Knight, 2010). That is, the individuals who create side effects at that point will in general keep on perpetrating wrongdoing or withdrawn conduct.

Numerous teenagers with CDs show ASB in adulthood (Burke et al., 2010; Khalifa et al., 2012). Be that as it may, on the grounds that a few kids determined to have ODD don't encounter increasingly hostile to social manifestations from CD (Burke et al., 2010), not every single youngsters with Disc will keep on indicating ASB until adulthood (Holmes et al., 2001). In spite of the fact that the hazard factors for ODD and CD (Goldstein et al., 2012; Khalifa et al., 2012) are like those for PPE (Lahey and

Loeber, 1997; Simonoff et al., 2004), youths with CD and the sky is the limit from there. The event of PPE (without manifestations of youth ODD) will in general be increasingly hard to process negative feelings, fears, and indications of enduring in others. They likewise have all the earmarks of being progressively intrepid and precarious, have less dread, less subjective shortages, are increasingly forceful and dismiss ordinary qualities and respond inadequately to discipline. Be that as it may, individuals without ADD indications will in general grow up (Frick, 2012; Frick and White, 2008). Teenage CD additionally have an expanded danger of liquor maltreatment at a youthful age (Howard et al., 2011; Khalifa et al., 2012).

PERSONALITY DISORDER

Side effects of APD for the most part decline with expanding age (Goldstein et al., 2012). In spite of this reality, APD as a rule endures forever. Studies show that grown-ups determined to have APD are bound to become guardians when they are youngsters or at a youthful age. powerless against destitution; expanded paces of medication misuse, suicide, demise, challenges in looking after work, higher separation rates and relationship issues, explanations behind utilizing state help programs and saw low personal satisfaction; and condemned to numerous years in jail (Farris et al., 2011; Goldstein et al., 2012; Olino et al., 2010; Walters and Knight, 2010).

The indications of BPD and related issue change significantly from individual to individual, with the best unsteadiness and drive control seen plainly in early adulthood. Side effects will in general diminishing with age, and the danger of suicide likewise diminishes when individuals with BPD are in center and late adulthood. The vast majority with BPD accomplish more prominent utilitarian solidness in the third and fourth many years of life (APA, 2013). The individuals who were determined to have BPD and who gotten some degree of treatment gave some positive outcomes. 88% of grown-ups in mental medical clinics determined to have BPD show symptomatic abatement inside 10 years, with practically half (39.3%) improving inside two years in the wake of being released. The individuals who have been analyzed and treated in adulthood are bound to reduction and have less wounds to kids (Zanarini et al., 2006).

OTHER DISORDERS

All in all, psychological issue seem to diminish after some time. Conduct issue seem to diminish during pubescence and adulthood among those determined to have mental imbalance range issue. It has been seen that specific bungled practices, for example, irregular or repeating propensities and careless conduct, show a critical diminishing with age and the impression of general destructivity will in general decline. Improved conduct is bound to happen in individuals with more positive passage conduct in teenagers and in individuals without associative psychological disorder (Shattuck et al., 2007). So also, patients with Tourette's disorder frequently experience a noteworthy decrease in dangerous side effects after some time, with more than 33% encountering total abatement (Bloch and Leckman, 2009). This is a confusion wherein psychological disorder are not diminished in adulthood. Despite the fact that IED side effects typically show up before the age of 40 years, the fundamental highlights as a rule stay for a considerable length of time (APA, 2013), albeit an abatement in specific manifestations can be seen after some time (Kessler et al., 2006)).

For individuals with serious intellectual handicaps, particularly the individuals who have comorbid psychological disorder, mental issue stay a significant issue and are significant as far as lodging needs (McIntyre et al., 2002). In patients with bipolar disorder, the recurrence of mental hospitalizations because of bipolar disorder in adulthood is higher than inpatient pediatric clinics, albeit damaging manifestations will in general be less hyper and maniacal (Bladder and Carlson, 2007). Since DMDD is another ailment, there is as of now no exploration on its advancement into adulthood.

Psychological disorders are surprising and can stop a whole person's life. The majority of these disarranges have a few reasons for youth with critical comorbidities between these scatters. Side effects are many, if not all, of this issue indicating dynamic reduction in adulthood, in spite of the fact that those with progressively serious side effects in youth will in general show increasingly relentless side effects in adulthood. While thinking about the manifestations, advancement, and course of the confusion, it is commonly imperative to think about the seriousness and setting of the turmoil as a manual for understanding the predominance, travel, and care needs of individuals with Psychological disorder.

CHAPTER FIVE
CORE SYMPTOMS OF DISRUPTIVE PSYCHOLOGICAL DISORDERS

ATTENTION DEFICIENCY HYPERACTIVITY DISORDER (ADHD)

ADHD is portrayed by a degree of heedlessness, extreme action and insufficient impulsivity which significantly affects different territories of day by day life (for example family communications, peer connections, scholastic accomplishment). . As per the fifth release of the Manual for the American Mental Relationship for the Conclusion and Measurements of Mental Issue (DSM-5, 2013), criteria for ADHD in youths require some careless or hyperactive/hasty side effects that happen at 12 years old. at any rate in two conditions and restrain or decrease the nature of social, scholarly or proficient capacities. The DSM-5 characterizes ADHD as three sorts: joined introductions, generally careless introductions and most hyperactive/imprudent introductions. What's more, DSM-5 requires a sign of the seriousness of ADHD (for example gentle, moderate, or extreme).

ANALYTIC AND DIAGNOSIS CONSIDERATION

ADHD is frequently connected with other Psychological disorder, which can make ADHD appear to be unique from individual to individual. For instance, half - 60% of young people with ADHD meet criteria for restriction issue, 30% for comorbid conduct issue and up to 25% for uneasiness or state of mind issue (Jensen et al., 2001). Likewise, ADHD manifestations seem to build up; The hyperactive/indiscreet prevailing introduction regularly happens in preschool, while the introduction which is for the most part careless is frequently determined to have expanding age (Lahey et al., 2005).

DISSEMINATION AND ITS COURSE

ADHD is one of the most widely recognized mental ailments in youth and influences 5% of school-age young people around the world (Faraone et al., 2003) with up to multiple times the demonstrative recurrence of men than ladies in network based examples (Barkley, 2006). What's more, ADHD is presently viewed as an incessant condition that influences numerous youngsters as they develop. Given the changing appearance of ADHD in youngsters after some time and the frequently watched mental comorbid conditions and incessant nature of ADHD, treatment is regularly multimodal and requires dynamic association from numerous professionals and key people in human life. The focal point of this section is to audit the writing on pharmacological, psychosocial, and mix ways to deal with treating ADHD in kids, youths, and grown-ups.

PHARMACOLOGICAL TREATMENT

As per the American Foundation of Pediatrics (AAP) Quality Improvement Council measures and Substance/Hyperactivity Subcommittee (AAP, 2011), specialists are prescribed to regard ADHD as a constant condition and ought to suggest energizers as a feature of a fitting treatment the board plan notwithstanding psychosocial care. The utilization of energizers has been perceived as the best quality level for the consideration of youngsters with ADHD, and there are numerous investigations that demonstrate this status. As of late, a few classes of new medications have risen as elective medicines to treat ADHD side effects. In the previous 15 years there has been a developing and solid writing on pharmacological consideration for young people and grown-ups with ADHD.

STIMULANTS MEDICATION

Stimulants are the primary decision for pharmacological treatment of ADHD in school-age youths. About 70% of kids who use stimulants show an expansion in side effects, making them the most usually recommended treatment (AAP, 2011). Methylphenidate (MPH) specifically is the most generally utilized stimulant (Mohammadi and Akhondzadeh, 2011). MPH was at first just accessible as momentary direct discharge (IR) (Ritalin). While this definition has been demonstrated compelling in preschool kids (Greenhill et al., 2006a), school-age youngsters (Abikoff et al., 2004) and youths (Evans et al., 2001), it is better than different medications . .) and for grown-ups (Retz et al., 2011) short half-life is a significant detriment. Hence, slow discharge definitions have been created to lessen hindrances to consistence with some day by day organization (Wolraich et al., 2001).

Various broadened MPH discharge plans are at present accessible. For instance, OROS-MPH is a solitary oral portion, a solitary controlled osmotic portion intended to keep up the adequacy of a medication over a 12 hour time frame (Wolraich et al., 2001). In like manner, Ritalin LA (ER-MPH utilizing a circular oral medication conveyance framework) mirrors MPH-IR two times per day, with Metadate CD (MPH utilizing Diffucaps innovation) giving 30% quick medication and the staying 70% above despite the fact that each medication these differ in their pharmacokinetic properties, all of which contain a similar dynamic fixings, MPH, and work by guaranteeing that the plasma convergence of MPX keeps on expanding because of time discharge innovation. A few randomized controlled preliminaries have demonstrated that this class of medications is powerful, safe, and mediocre for younger students, youths, and grown-ups with ADHD (Spencer et al., 2011; Wilens et al., 2006a; Wolraich et al. ., 2001). , despite the fact that the impacts in the example from teenagers and grown-ups seem to have debilitated contrasted with more youthful kids (Harsh et al., 2012). The oral discharge MPH detailing is commonly very much endured. Normal symptoms incorporate cerebral pains, stomach throbs, anorexia, a sleeping disorder, and torpidity. A large portion of these reactions are accounted for to be mellow and happen in under 10% of study members (Wolraich et al., 2001).

Methylphenidate is likewise accessible in a transdermal definition (Daytrana). At present endorsed by the US Nourishment and Medication Organization for use in kids ages 6 to 12 years with ADHD. Research has exhibited the advantages of transdermal structures (for example Pelham et al., 2005). As far as anyone is concerned, an examination (Findling et al., 2010) found that transdermal MPH is viable in youths with ADHD dependent on the improvement of ADHD side effects in clinical medication surveys. Marchant et al. (2011) additionally found noteworthy advantages of transdermal MPH in grown-ups with ADHD. Strikingly, this examination found that transdermal MBC was similarly as successful in grown-ups with ADHD alone, ADHD in addition to passionate dysregulation, ADHD in addition to inverse pressure issue, and those with ADHD in addition to enthusiastic dysregulation and inverse issue. The portion is surrendered in patches for to eight hours (Chavez et al., 2009). The upside of this delivery strategy is that it is an option for youngsters who can't swallow enormous pills. Also, the term of the restorative impact relies upon the period of time the fix is utilized, which offers adaptability in the length of the impact (Wilens et al., 2008). Misfortunes from transdermal piece incorporate more slow beginning of activity and danger of skin aggravation (McGough et al., 2005). Opposite reactions detailed are like every single other type of RBM, including diminished craving, cerebral pains, and sleep deprivation.

At long last, MPH is likewise accessible in an artificially adjusted variant of the medication dexmethylphenidate (d-MPH; focalin). MPH is a blend of two isomers: dextrose (d) threo methylphenidate and levo (1) treometilfenidate. 1-isomers can hypothetically contribute less to the helpful impact of MPH than d-isomers, so organization of d-isomers in separation can permit lower portions at a similar level of adequacy (Chavez et al., 2009); Mohammadi and Akhondzadeh, 2011). It is affirmed by the FDA in kids with ADHD more than 6 years and is accessible in a moderate discharge plan that works quick and is all around endured (d-MPH-ER). Randomized controlled preliminaries have indicated that d-MPH-ER is better than fake treatment (Childress et al., 2009); additionally demonstrated that d-MPH-ER has a quicker beginning of activity of OROS-MPH (Muniz et al., 2008; Silva et al., 2008). Here additionally, the symptom profile is like other MPH measurements structures.

Modafinil has likewise been accounted for to soothe ADHD indications in school-matured kids. It is right now endorsed for the treatment of narcolepsy since it has been appeared to build consideration. The FDA is right now not affirmed for ADHD treatment. Since it has a generally little hurtful impact and nearly doesn't mess dependence up, it isn't viewed as a controlled substance. Randomized controlled preliminaries (RCTs) have indicated that Modafinil lessens ADHD side effects superior to fake treatment at home and at school (Greenhill et al., 2006b). As far as anyone is concerned, just one investigation contrasted Modafinil legitimately and MPH and found comparative outcomes as far as adequacy in lessening manifestations between the two medications (Amiri et al., 2008). Modafinil symptoms typically incorporate sleep deprivation, diminished craving and cerebral stress.

BENEFITS OF PHARMACOTHERAPY TREATMENT OF ADHD

With numerous choices for reasonable discharge details, this medication is the main treatment for ADHD that is alluring on the grounds that the time has come devouring and economical. Individuals take one portion promptly in the day and use it for the duration of the day. What's more, medicate treatment has been demonstrated to viably diminish the basic side effects, improve working and work in school, and improve personal satisfaction (Huang and Tsai, 2011; Surman et al., 2013). Apparently, pharmacotherapy can be less expensive, in any event for the time being, than without treatment or treatment alone (Wu et al., 2012).

Be that as it may, reactions, including loss of hunger, cerebral pains, weight reduction, a sleeping disorder, sluggishness, development impediment and hypertension, happen in 10-30% of youngsters who take medicine to treat ADHD indications (Huang and Tsai, 2011). Adherence to treatment regimens is additionally frequently imperfect (Chacko et al., 2010). Despite the fact that medication use is related with an expansion in state administered tests, it isn't related with a consistent increment in school capabilities leaving or with the standardization of scholastic working (Langberg and Becker, 2012). What's more, guardians frequently incline toward social treatment as opposed to treatment alone, and conduct treatment and blend drugs have been demonstrated to be better than unimodal treatment (Pelham, 1999), particularly in the mind boggling introduction of ADHD (Hinshaw and Arnold, 2014). At long last, there are no convincing information to show the long haul advantages of a pharmacological way to deal with treating ADHD in young people. Young people and grown-ups with ADHD think that its exceptionally hard to stick to treatment (Chacko et al., 2010; Olfson et al., 2007), and there are frequently leftover issue that require extra treatment.

PSYCHOLOGICAL TREATMENT OF ADHD

Given the upkeep of antagonistic long haul impacts after the discontinuance of pharmacological treatment (Hoza et al., 2005), countless individuals who experience symptoms from prescription treatment for ADHD (see Chacko et al., 2010) stay with the Pharmacological Consideration injuries. Care and open worry about the long haul obscure impacts of supported energizer use have a basic requirement for proof based psychosocial care for ADHD. This worry is exceptionally clear given the expanding number of ADHD cases in preschool age, and the writing mirrors an expanded enthusiasm for intercessions for this populace (Rajwan et al., 2012).

We do that from Evans et al. (2014), intercessions to conduct the executives mediations (intercessions that show individuals other than the patient's capacity to change persistent conduct in setting) and preparing mediations (intercessions that straightforwardly learn/center around target patients to be improved) Abilities) just as a mix of these intercessions. Social administration intercessions for the most part incorporate conduct preparing for guardians, conduct the executives for cohorts, and conduct mediations for peers, which are all basically utilized in preschool kids with ADHD. Learning mediations incorporate a progression of intercessions, including conventional social aptitudes preparing, authoritative abilities preparing, neurocognitive consideration, and intellectual conduct mediations that have been learned in school age teenagers by ADHD grown-ups. General outline of the most recent RCT results, if accessible, for each sort of psychosocial mediation that incorporates preschool youngsters through grown-ups with ADHD.

At long last, intercessions focusing on couples/grown-ups with ADHD can likewise have a spot in ADHD psychosocial care. Despite the fact that this intercession has not been generally considered and no RCT is known to date, 40% - 60% of kids and teenagers with ADHD keep on having noteworthy ADHD indications and related development. The individuals who care for grown-ups with ADHD can consistently discover circumstances where such mediations can be useful.

BEHAVIORAL ADMINISTRATION INTERCESSIONS
Behavioral Training For Guardians

Behavioral Parent Training (BPT) is an intercession that means to help guardians of preschool or school-matured youngsters with ADHD work as risky practices (e.g., rebelliousness, trouble finishing errands, and so on.) comprehend and afterward learn explicit strategies to change precursors and results identified with the event of tricky objective conduct to build the recurrence and seriousness of this current objective's conduct. Advantage arranged techniques incorporate, for instance, setting house rules and utilizing compelling requests, while outcome situated strategies incorporate exceptionally stamped applause, arranged negligence and sitting tight for uplifting feedback. There are likewise techniques that utilization the two strategies and spotlight on advantages and outcomes. For instance, the Day by day Detailing Card (DRC) is an observing and upkeep framework that is regularly utilized in BPT and capacities as a school-to-home correspondence framework to improve school conduct. Law based Republic of the Congo centers around the recognizable proof and operational meaning of target conduct and moderate objectives. It offers various prizes when the kid arrives at a middle of the road objective, just as ramifications for accomplishing a moderate objective. It is significant that significant grown-ups (guardians and educators) reliably screen progress towards objectives and change middle of the road objectives dependent on mediation reactions in the Fair Republic of Congo. The BPT technique is regularly considered through a shared model in which the specialist works with guardians to talk about the BPT strategy and to adjust the technique to explicit family conditions. BPT arrives in various configurations, including gatherings, parent-youngster two-digit arrangements, and parent-kid group of three specialists. Most BPT mediations are a couple of hour sessions that happen each week for around eight to twelve weeks. In BPT intercessions, different strategies are regularly used to help parental BPT preparing, including direct exercises, discourses, video guidelines, displaying advisor techniques, pretending with guardians and direct practice of BPT strategies with kids during preparing in sessions. Numerous BPT programs that emphasis on an assortment of conduct issues are commonly accessible, and some are planned explicitly for social issues that are frequently connected with ADHD manifestations (e.g., Barkley, 2013; Kapalka, 2007).

Randomized clinical preliminaries reliably show that BPT is one of the best psychosocial intercessions for ADHD regarding the impacts of intense treatment on essential results (Pelham and Fabiano, 2008). RCTs from different BPT programs show a decrease in ADHD side effects and brokenness (Anastopoulos et al., 1993; Chacko et al., 2009; Fabiano et al., 2012). Albeit most BPT programs are assessed all in all, Kapalka's (2007) is analyzed with a different RCT to check the viability of each program step (for an audit see Kapalka, 2010). Most GMP programs urge all parental figures to take an interest in this program, since care will in general improve in such circumstances.

Furthermore, an ongoing BPT study concentrated on change in proof based treatment that prompts expanded access and inclusion for treatment of hazard populaces (for example single parents, Chacko et al., 2009; Fathers, Fabiano et al., 2009, 2012). Moreover, BPT has been appeared to diminish parental pressure (Chacko et al., 2009), improve parental welfare (Anastopoulos et al., 1993) and improve childcare conduct (Chacko et al., 2009; Fabiano et al., 2012). .). For adolescents, parent-high schooler coordinated effort has demonstrated to be a promising way to deal with expanding family struggle, as opposed to working straightforwardly with guardians to manage startling circumstances through BPT. With this methodology, guardians and adolescents learn relational abilities, distinguish existing ineffectual correspondence practices, and work to tackle issues by methodically utilizing powerful relational abilities (Barkley et al., 2001).

BEHAVIORAL CLASSES

Mediations for study hall conduct the board are other built up techniques for the treatment of preschool and school-matured youngsters with ADHD (Pelham and Fabiano, 2008). Like BPT, the focal point of social intercessions in study hall the board is to comprehend the capacity of conduct issues in schools/study halls and to alter the signs and results related with the development of distinguished objective practices. As per what BPT instructs to guardians, instructors are regularly urged to utilize techniques that will before long be accessible (for example Rules for educating, compelling directions) and strategies that emphasis on results (for example acclaim, sitting tight for encouraging feedback).

It is significant that execution Compelling conduct mediations in the administration of exercises require close coordinated effort among advisor and educator. Homerooms fluctuate in size, number of understudies with social issues and assets. As in working with guardians at BPT, compelling joint effort and adjustment of mediation techniques for the extraordinary needs of instructors and the study hall condition are urgent for the effective execution and reaction of social intercessions in study hall the executives.

Conduct class intercessions explicitly intended for ADHD issues incorporate the day by day declaration referenced above, just as organized projects that look like BPT programs intended for guardians (for example Kapalka, 2009). They are utilized in ordinary homerooms (Kapalka, 2010; Miranda et al., 2002), unique study halls (Fabiano et al., 2010) and study halls in summer programs (Fabiano et al., 2004). Studies show that this mediation prompts a huge increment in ADHD manifestations evaluated by guardians and instructors (Miranda et al., 2002); In any case, this outcome isn't constantly watched (Fabiano et al., 2010). Studies have indicated an increasingly steady increment in non-ADHD psychological disorder, with kids accepting crisis the board demonstrating a huge increment in study hall consistence and an expansion in accomplishment of conduct objectives (Fabiano et al., 2010). Huge decreases in the frequency and seriousness of psychological disorder (over the top impulsive issue/conduct issue; Fabiano et al., 2004, 2010; Kapalka, 2010;) and animosity (Fabiano et al., 2004). A few investigations have indicated enhancements in scholastic execution (Fabiano et al., 2010), decrease of learning issues and improved outcomes in arithmetic and science (Miranda et al., 2002); Be that as it may, social possibility the executives regularly doesn't altogether improve scholarly execution. It ought to be noticed that an ongoing meta-investigation of school care for youngsters with ADHD shows that this mediation has a moderate to enormous impact on school conduct and results, and that school intercessions ought to be essential consideration for understudies with ADHD (DuPaul et al. ., 2012a).

CONDUCT MEDIATION FOR PEERS

Behavioral conduct also tends to fundamentally improve peer connections, a region with huge inabilities for youngsters with ADHD. In an ongoing report by Mikami et al. (2012) educators utilize conduct the executives, including acclaim, singular consideration, and acknowledgment messages from others, to expand shared acknowledgment in the homerooms of their friends without ADHD. Albeit social issues just changed marginally, trial kids with the ADHD preliminary were altogether less dismissed by their companions, had progressively common kinship, and got increasingly positive companion messages toward the finish of the program than their ADHD companions in the benchmark group. This shows the social administration systems utilized by educators can build terrible associations with peers. In like manner, Mikami et al. (2010) trains guardians to become social mentors for their kids, which carries their kids to unexpected conditions for prosocial conduct. Contrasted and those in the untreated treatment control gathering, the treated subjects demonstrated a huge increment in parental social abilities and nature of play, and educators who didn't think about the arrangement of treatment additionally revealed an expansion in compassion. furthermore, peer acknowledgment. This examination shows that social aptitudes outside of human services are expanding and changes are accounted for by individuals who don't know treatment.

COMPETENCY BASED INTERVENTIONS

In this segment, we see "expertise based intercessions" which center legitimately around educating patients about specific abilities to manage the fundamental zones of brokenness (social issues, disruption, trouble in driving, and so forth.). This mediation centers around breaking down complex utilitarian zones of discrete undertakings/abilities and utilizing systems to prepare patients in discrete aptitudes through different strategies (for example remedial displaying, pretend, and so on.). Criticism, observing of abilities in the regular habitat (for example school, home, network) and support are frequently significant perspectives to guarantee compelling usage of aptitudes. The consequences of different investigations on competency-based learning have given blended outcomes relying upon the focal point of the mediation.

Customary mediations identified with social abilities regularly incorporate uncommon directions for youngsters about different parts of social aptitudes (for instance, eye to eye connection, satisfactory individual flexibility of discourse, certainty, and so on.). In light of the present writing, conventional preparing in social aptitudes is viewed as sketchy (Pelham and Fabiano, 2008). The absence of significant exact proof for this sort of intercession can be identified with contrasts in the span or length of treatment, just as the power and substance of the mediation itself in the examination.

Abikoff et al. (2012) built up a hierarchical intercession for preparing school-age youth with ADHD. This intercession centers around instructing kids to utilize new apparatuses and techniques to record assignments, compose learning material, screen task time all the more successfully, and separation bigger errands into littler ones. overseen. Guardians and instructors must acclaim kids for their authoritative aptitudes. The consequences of randomized clinical preliminaries show that the individuals who got the mediation got a much better hierarchical rating contrasted with the holding up list, as expressed by guardians and educators, just as improved scholarly working, schoolwork and family struggle.

Noteworthy endeavors have likewise been made to show the capacities of young people and teenagers with ADHD for certain useful issue. Langberg et al. (2012) adjusted authoritative intercessions for youngsters with optional ADHD, with results showing a critical increment in development and quarterly follow-up in parent appraisals of association, schoolwork, and family struggle. Likewise, the focal point of research is on showing driving aptitudes in youth (Fabiano et al., 2011) and improving scholarly readiness (Meyer and Kelley, 2008; Sibley et al., 2013). It is significant that significant grown-ups, (for example, guardians or instructors) cooperate for ADHD adolescents and bolster youth in settings where these youngsters must utilize the abilities they have learned. Incapacity abilities mediations are to be sure a promising strategy for intercession, particularly for teenagers and youths.

CBSBI (Cognitive Behavioral Skills Intervention) is by all accounts a promising methodology for grown-ups with ADHD (Knouse and Safren, 2013). CBSI recognizes clear and operationally characterized treatment objectives, trailed by utilitarian examination to see how issues emerge that influence patients' capacity to effectively accomplish their objectives. Utilitarian investigation must prompt the determination of techniques to evacuate hindrances to accomplishing the patient's objectives. Endeavors to utilize the distinguished system additionally require the advisor to recognize and treat generally watched negative information (e.g. Indications of progress/disappointment, win big or bust, and so forth.) and feelings (e.g. outrage). Patient's endeavors to apply that solitary joined by aptitudes. Also, CBSBI incorporates psychoeducation for ADHD, endeavors to assist grown-ups with ADHD stick to treatment plans, utilize noteworthy others (assuming any) to help the utilization of aptitudes and treat repeat.

Information from two randomized clinical preliminaries bolster the CBSBI approach in the treatment of ADHD in grown-ups. Safren et al. (2010) contrasted CBSBI singular mediations and loosened up preparing and instructive help for 86 grown-ups with ADHD. The outcomes demonstrated that CBSBI mediations delivered a more prominent increment in ADHD indications that were kept up for a year of development. Solanto et al. (2010) contrasted the CBSBI intercession gathering and the care group of 88 grown-ups with ADHD and furthermore found that CBSBI mediation brought about a more prominent improvement in ADHD manifestations. Generally speaking, the outcomes from these two enormous randomized clinical preliminaries show that CBSBI is a reasonable treatment for ADHD in grown-ups.

Endeavors have likewise been made to look at other competency-based intercessions for grown-ups with ADHD. Consideration arranged intercessions mean to improve discovery of inward conditions and give individuals better command over their conduct/responses. For grown-ups with ADHD, it is prescribed that better location of natural conditions will give better authority over consideration, impulsivity, and normal issues that happen in grown-ups with ADHD (e.g. disposition). Zylowska et al. (2008) and Philipsen et al. (2007) assessed intercessions that concentrated on care preparing in two open clinical investigations. Information from this examination show that this sort of intercession can improve ADHD manifestations in grown-ups. Be that as it may, due to the examination structure, stricter checks are required.

Notwithstanding care based intercessions, ADHD preparing has become a generally utilized methodology. The National ADHD Asset Center portrays this preparation as "when one individual (mentor) gives target input and direction in a sorted out and systematic approach to help other people (customers) manage issues or arrive at explicit objectives of accomplishing" (http:/www. help4adhd.org/day by day/mentor). Albeit some open preliminaries have been completed solely with ADHD preparing (e.g., Kubik et al., 2010) and preparing with CBSBI (e.g. Stevenson et al., 2003), with starter results that affect a few zones. with practical issue, ADHD plainly requires a progressively thorough appraisal of ADHD preparing.

NEUROCOGNITIVE CONSIDERATION

Given the expanded acknowledgment of neurocognitive shortages in young people with ADHD and the job of these components in the long haul course of ADHD (Halperin and Shultz, 2006), there is an expanded enthusiasm for neurocognitive preparing for ADHD treatment. Cogmed Work Memory Training (CWMT) has pulled in exceptional enthusiasm for examine and clinical networks on account of the quantity of randomized clinical preliminaries that have researched this mediation to treat ADHD in teenagers (see Chacko et al., 2013, a diagram of this investigation).). Numerous RCTs have given a few advantages from CWMT, particularly in connection to parental side effects of ADHD and working memory assignments, which are fundamentally the same as CWMT preparing errands (for example consequences of close moves). There is no CWMT-RCT overview that shows an expansion in daze evaluator appraisals. In the as of late finished RCT, Chacko et al. (2014), utilizing a progressively controlled fake treatment infection, found the same CWMT consequences for parent/educator reports about ADHD indications, target proportions of consideration, lack of caution and action, or scholarly execution results. The absence of a noteworthy impact of CWMT is predictable with the general outcomes found in neurocognitive intercession examines in youths (school-age young people) with ADHD (Affinity et al., 2013). Affinity et al. In a meta-investigation of neurocognitive mediations in youths with ADHD, they found that these intercessions had no impact on ADHD results. As far as anyone is concerned, just three investigations have inspected the impacts of neurocognitive preparing in grown-ups with ADHD (Harsh et al., 2014; Virta et al., 2010; White and Shah, 2006). As a rule, this investigation found a few advantages of neurocognitive mediations for chose neurocognitive end focuses, yet no broad impacts on ADHD indications or clutters identified with day by day life capacities have been found. Generally speaking, it is promising that neurocognitive intercessions will change the pathophysiology hidden ADHD and lead to increasingly practical treatment impacts. This remaining parts a prolific report territory; In any case, information propose that present neurocognitive mediations ought not be viewed as first or second-line treatment for ADHD in young people or grown-ups.

Neurofeedback training additionally got extraordinary consideration as an intercession in the treatment of ADHD. In spite of the fact that there are numerous uncontrolled neurofeedback thinks about, a few controlled RCTs have been led. In an ongoing RCT,

Gevensleben et al. (2009) found critical advantages from neurofield returns on ADHD, ODD and parental hostility, just as instructor appraisals for ADHD. It is significant that there are no critical impacts of neurofeedback on social, scholarly, and home capacities, and the impacts of neurofeedback have all the earmarks of being altogether littler than those found for both pharmacological and conduct ways to deal with treat ADHD.

Similarly, Steiner et al. (2014a, 2014b) found the advantages of Neurofield for school-age youths with ADHD, yet were like Gevensleben et al. (2009) their belongings are less contrasted with psychosocial and pharmacological ways to deal with ADHD treatment. It is fascinating, in any case, that in ex-post assessments, youngsters endowed with neurofeedback have encountered a persistent improvement in the working of youngsters who are under intellectual preparing or control. This tenacious impact is significant in light of the fact that ADHD is a ceaseless condition and mediations that expansion after some time are significant for treating ADHD. Neurofeedback has likewise been concentrated in grown-ups with ADHD. Except for uncontrolled gathering considers (e.g. Mayer et al., 2012), the accessible writing contains just contextual analyses. In spite of the fact that this is promising, more research is required before the job of neurofield return in the treatment of ADHD can be completely assessed. Neurofeedback is maybe best observed as a viable second-line treatment for ADHD in teenagers. No ends can be drawn about the sufficiency of Neurofeedback as a treatment choice for grown-ups.

INTERCESSION WITH PARTNERS

Adult couples with ADHD regularly experience huge

pressure and dissatisfaction when managing numerous issues in their every day lives identified with ADHD indications. Murphy and Barkley (1996) report that couples determined to have ADHD as couples frequently experience serious disappointment in their marriage. Couples frequently feel confounded, furious, and disappointed, and gripe that their accomplices are awful, muddled, distracted, questionable, childish, unfeeling, and flippant audience members. Barkley (2006) recommends that couples must discover that a considerable lot of these issues may not be because of "deliberate damage" in light of the fact that such a large amount of this conduct can be straightforwardly identified with ADHD side effects (p. 699). Rather, joining forces with individuals with ADHD needs to comprehend the world from their accomplice's point of view, quit accusing them, and join them to battle the "shared adversary" (ADHD manifestations). At the point when the two accomplices create common comprehension about how ADHD side effects influence the relationship, what each accomplice needs from the other, and that joint effort altogether improves the relationship, the possibility of expanding positive results (Dixon, 1995). Despite the fact that there are scarcely any assets for specialists who explicitly manage this strategy, some have as of late gotten accessible (e.g. Kapalka, 2010; Ramsay and Rostain, 2008).

A few examinations have observationally researched the advantages of this mediation. In any case, a few examinations have indicated that hitched or double directing improves the manifestations hidden ADHD in "recognized patients" and lessens the weight all in all family. Nadeau (1995) suggests that double care be remembered for generally speaking ADHD the executives, and Hallowell (1995) found that consideration of an accomplice improves the general result in the treatment of grown-ups with ADHD. Ratey et al. (1995) announced that accomplice directing decreases side effects, diminish pressure, and increment closeness to families determined to have ADHD in couples.

ADVANTAGES PSYCHOTHERAPY FOR TREATMENT

All in all, the ebb and flow condition of research on psychosocial treatment for ADHD underpins parental conduct preparing, social possibility the board and social mediations as connections as viable intercessions for the treatment of ADHD in youths of preschool age and school age. Some preparation intercessions have all the earmarks of being of huge effectiveness for teenagers and more established young people (e.g., preparing authoritative aptitudes) and grown-ups (CBSBI), while some stay promising (e.g. Neurofeedback), others neglect to be controlled experimentally (e.g. mediations neurocognitive) and others plainly require increasingly exact appraisal (e.g. training).

Psychosocial care profits by showing key capabilities to scratch grown-ups (i.e. guardians and educators) just as youngsters and grown-ups who can diminish handicaps related with ADHD side effects. When these abilities are aced, they can hypothetically be utilized in various settings every now and then. It is significant that there are no potential wellbeing dangers related with psychosocial mediations, albeit some iatrogenic impacts have been accounted for. Barkley et al. (2001) found that 10% of guardians of dyadic adolescents who were relegated BPT had post-treatment impedances. These discoveries underscore the significance of expert consideration and screen treatment progress. Guardians truly like psychosocial intercessions to treat ADHD (Pelham, 1999), which makes it a first-line mediation from the point of view of numerous guardians.

Notwithstanding, the restriction of utilizing psychosocial care as the main methodology is that care requires continuous and moderately concentrated organization (mediations must be completed a few hours per week) and will in general be costly (contrasted with pharmacological intercessions). Similarly as with pharmacological methodologies, there is no proof that intense dosages of social intercessions have an additionally enduring impact on results in young people with ADHD, in spite of the fact that exploration shows that advantages can proceed for a while after treatment is halted (Barkley, 2006) and treatment can likewise be related long haul pressure decrease, evidently at home. The long haul consequences of psychosocial care for young people and grown-ups are constrained. Intercessions, for example, neurocognitive preparing and neurofeedback can, in any case, offer chances to improve results after treatment. This is as yet theoretical and requires further examination. A noteworthy impediment, as found by AAP (2011), is that in certain networks there is a lack of specialists who know about conduct intercessions for youths with ADHD, making it hard for families to acknowledge this proof based mediation. This may happen with psychosocial care (i.e. CBSBI) for grown-ups with ADHD.

COMBINED TREATMENT

Hypothetically, many contend that consolidated pharmacological and psychosocial intercessions are the best treatment for ADHD (Pelham et al., 2000). Various broad examinations have been done to efficiently evaluate the blend of pharmacological and psychosocial medicines - just in school-age youngsters with ADHD. As far as anyone is concerned, sadly there are no orderly surveys of a blend of pharmacological and psychosocial medications for youths or grown-ups with ADHD.

Klein et al. (2004) considered kids matured 7 to 9 years who were determined to have ADHD without comorbid preparing or social issue. Kids are separated into three treatment nations: MPH just, MPH in addition to escalated Multimodal Psychosocial Treatment (MPT) and MPH in addition to psychosocial care consideration (ACT). At the point when acknowledged, all kids were sedate free at section and accomplished a critical increment in the five-week RBM study. Youngsters, guardians and instructors take part in care at MPT. Kids get singular scholastic help, authoritative and social aptitudes preparing and singular psychotherapy. Guardians go to BPT and guiding sessions, and the educators fill occasions to report school conduct and scholastic advancement. At ACT, youngsters complete non-scholarly individual and gathering undertakings and partake in outside play instead of accepting scholastic and authoritative preparing. Kids get general help at home, however no individual appraisal of scholastic aptitudes is assessed or techniques for improving scholarly abilities are examined (Klein et al., 2004).

One year results demonstrated that the treatment bunch didn't discover various impacts regarding manifestations, capacity, issue or side effect edge (Abikoff et al., 2004) just as scholarly execution, household conduct or enthusiastic pressure (Hechtman) et al., 2004a) between treatment gathering. Likewise, after the primary year, it was accounted for that all youngsters, paying little mind to the treatment gathering, encountered a repeat in the wake of changing from MPH to fake treatment. At long last, Hechtman et al. (2004b) detailed the impacts of various medications on childcare rehearses. The outcomes demonstrated that the MPH in addition to MPT bunch had far superior information on social standards and subsequently a critical bit of leeway in accomplishing instructive objectives than the MPH bunch alone or the MPH in addition to ACT gathering. In the principal year, be that as it may, there were the same impacts as treatment on the size of child rearing practices or kids' view of child rearing practices. In the subsequent year, moms of kids in the IPH-in addition to MPT bunch were delegated having obviously better data about social standards than moms of youngsters in the IPH-in addition to AST gathering. Moms in the gathering with MPH alone didn't contrast altogether from moms in the gathering with MPH in addition to X-ray. Likewise, there are the same impacts as the treatment of the degree of child rearing practices or the youngster's impression of the child rearing practices found. By and large, there is no proof of the prevalence of MPH in addition to MPT looked at over MPH as far as childcare rehearses. One constraint of this investigation is the way that the medications in this examination didn't visually impaired guardians, educators, and specialists. Since every single youngsters must react to RBM to be remembered for this examination, this outcome will in general be a more steady MPH impact than that found in the more broad ADHD youthful populace.

The investigation by MTA Helpful Gathering (1999) is viewed as a remarkable examination in the investigation of ADHD treatment in youngsters. The analysts assessed youngsters matured 7 to 9.9 years (n = 579) who were determined to have the consolidated kind of ADHD. Members were partitioned into four gatherings: MPH just, psychosocial care just, MPH mix in addition to psychosocial care, or standard consideration in the network (which regularly included stimulative consideration). Concerning treatment, youngsters are first treated with various MPH portions and afterward the medication is custom fitted to the patient's needs. Under psychosocial conditions, members got 27 gathering sessions and 8 individual BPT sessions for about two months and a late spring consideration program (Pelham et al., 2000). Moreover, school care comprises of 10 to 16 week by week educator sessions that examine homeroom conduct the board procedures and 12 weeks of individual conduct work with youngsters to give input at school.

The outcomes have been accounted for in different distributions. In general, mix treatment and mediations identified with IPC alone didn't contrast clinically or factually regarding the degree of ADHD indication improvement, and both measurably just surpassed social treatment and outpatient care. For opposite end focuses -, for example, restriction side effects, disguise side effects, social abilities, parent-youngster connections, and scholarly capacities - just joint mediations are factually higher than network control status for certain endpoints (MTA Agreeable Gathering, 1999). Optional investigation shows that mix treatment is fundamentally superior to different medicines, with tantamount impact measures in the scope of 0.28 to 0.7 just for RBM or network control.

Given the clinical ramifications, there has been a lot of discussion about the understanding of MTA discoveries. For instance, Greene and Ablon (2001) report contrasts in the degree to which pharmacological and psychosocial medications have been adjusted to the necessities of kids. As to treatment, kids are first treated with various MPH portions and afterward the medication is changed in accordance with the patient's needs. Be that as it may, in psychosocial conditions, most angles continue as before, paying little heed to needs evaluation. All members got the equivalent social mediation bundle. Likewise, Pelham (1999) found that the fundamental 14-month result of the MTA study contrasted dynamic MPH and a blurring conduct mediation bundle (i.e., the force of social intercession was essentially diminished at quick development). Subsequently, a 14-month post-MTA examination isn't a precise gauge contrasting dynamic MPH and dynamic conduct mediations. While believing the measurement of intercessions to be thought about, the consequences of prompt treatment likewise show that blurring conduct mediations can have a significant effect.

The way that there is no distinction between conduct treatment for social mediations and standard practice in the network (a significant number of which acknowledge MPH) shows that social intercessions, regardless of whether not implemented, may equivalently affect MPCs that are effectively overseen in a network. It is intriguing that different examinations assessing joined pharmacological and psychosocial mediations have a more prominent subtlety that discloses the consolidated way to deal with treating ADHD. Others have demonstrated that when leading concentrated social intercessions, the outcomes have just restricted advantages from MPH (Pelham et al. 2005), or that MPH can be essentially decreased when utilized as a component of continuous social intercessions (Chacko et al. 2005) . 2005), which can be significant when considering long haul treatment for young people with ADHD.

ADVANTAGE OF COMBINED TREATMENT

Combined treatment (i.e. chose pharmacological and conduct intercessions) easily affects ADHD side effects and related issue in youths with ADHD. The joined methodology likewise offers the advantages offered by every methodology (e.g. building aptitudes, impacts in various utilitarian territories, and so on.). The joined methodology makes it conceivable to diminish the force of pharmacological and social intercessions, consequently giving a progressively handy model to long haul organization.

Be that as it may, as with multimodal intercession bundles, multifaceted nature is a restriction of its wide use. Giving the sort of concentrated conduct mediations utilized in the examination being analyzed requires a group of experts who arrange benefits in various conditions and times and include various partners (i.e. guardians, educators, and influenced youth). The capacity of routine specialist co-ops and frames of mind to actualize this sort of treatment routine is a basic issue, however it has not yet been examined.

Discussion on ADHD intercessions is extremely wide and keeps on developing. Despite the fact that the zone has distinguished various chosen mediations, there is a proceeding with enthusiasm for creating and assessing elective intercessions, on the grounds that there are no intercessions that have a general and enduring effect on all significant practical results that are regularly disturbed in individuals with ADHD. In this unique circumstance, future research must keep on assessing promising intercessions (e.g. neurofeedback, instructing, accomplice advising) that address the impediments of mediations that have incredible potential for ADHD treatment yet have not yet been demonstrated powerful (B (neurocognitive preparing) and further explore blends mediations that can have reciprocal impacts or reinforce utilitarian results. Specifically, the mix treatment writing for the treatment of young people and grown-ups with ADHD requires efficient evaluation.

Clinically, preschool and school-age kids are offered pharmacological and psychosocial medicines, explicitly explicit practices, which have clear and stable consequences for ADHD side effects and related issue, in any event in the present moment with dynamic treatment. Which intercession technique begins treatment (pharmacological or psychosocial or both) at what power/measurement and to what extent the treatment must be proceeded is a significant choice that requires dynamic investment of the patient, essential grown-up in the patient's life (e.g. guardians, instructors, life partner/accomplices) and specialist. Specifically, understanding grown-up inclinations and mentalities to execute social mediations is significant, in light of the fact that grown-ups today are essentially engaged with actualizing care. For youngsters, the writing shows that conduct based mediations that concentrate seriously in specific zones with utilitarian issue (e.g. culmination of schoolwork, association, and so on.) Bolster youngsters in learning certain aptitudes and trade approaches and backing from grown-ups (i.e. guardians and instructors) is a powerful approach. Likewise, CBSBI is a first-line ADHD mediation in quite a while, and CBSBI treatment rules are currently industrially accessible. Pharmacological intercessions are additionally successful in teenagers and grown-ups with ADHD. Be that as it may, medicine adherence (particularly over the long haul) is a noteworthy test for these gatherings. This shows when pharmacological treatment is utilized in this age gathering, endeavors are made to recognize obstructions to tranquilize consistence and synergistic endeavors.

CHAPTER SIX
OPPOSITIONAL DISRUPTIVE DISORDER (ODD)

Oppositional disruptive disorder (ODD) is a conduct issue that for the most part happens in kids and young people and comprises of a model of reaction of a contrary position that is immovably planted, purposeful resistance, upset state of mind and adverse consideration (Steiner et al., 2007; Stringaris) et al., 2010). Indicative and measurable manual for mental issue, fifth version (DSM-5; American Mental Affiliation [APA], 2013) reports that roughly 3.3% everything being equal and young people are influenced by ODD, with a future of 12.6% . Moreover, issues related with ODD regularly intensify fundamentally, and happen together with consideration shortfall/hyperactivity issue (ADHD), uneasiness issue and disposition issue (Martel et al., 2012). In view of their damaging nature and high comorbidity with different maladies, ODD issues influence the day by day working of individuals, yet additionally their associations with peers, relatives, instructors, and different guardians (Greene et al., 2002). In this manner, adequately assessing and defining fitting objectives for the treatment of ODD can be a complex clinical test and exertion.

DIAGNOSIS CONSIDERATION

As of now there are two primary classes of indications used to analyze ODD: outer social issues and negative feelings (Frick and Nigg, 2012). ODD was first remembered for the DSM-III in 1980 and requires at any rate two of the accompanying practices: minor infringement of the standards, fits, the capacity to think, provocative conduct, or determination (APA, 1980). Observational examination of this issue at that point prompts an extended portrayal of the indications (Angold and Costello, 1996; Stringaris et al., 2010). At present there are eight side effects of ODD recorded in DSM-5, including:

(1) Bantering with individuals or adults;
(2) Effectively declining to comply with the standards/prerequisites of power figures or dismissing it;
(3) Intentionally upsetting others;
(4) Reprimanding others for their own missteps or slip-ups;
(5) Powerless against being contacted, effectively irritated or somewhat irritating;
(6) Simple to lose discretion;
(7) Regularly irritated and furious; and
(8) Detestable or vindictive at any rate twice in a half year (APA, 2013, p. 462).

To think about a determination of ODD, at least four manifestations must be available for at any rate a half year. Manifestations should likewise show up with a recurrence and length that are commonly higher than practically identical practices in creating peers (i.e., adding to huge issues and disturbance of social, instructive, or proficient capacities). What's more, the primary ODD issues contrast from different conditions in that they frequently disregard the privileges of others.

Albeit ODD indications are not really normal in various circumstances, what's going on in the determination of DSM-5 is explicit to the seriousness of manifestations dependent on cross-circumstance handicap (Frick and Nigg, 2012). Consequently the analysis of ODD is delegated simple (restricted to one essential setting), moderate (accessible in at any rate two settings) and troublesome (accessible in at least three settings; APA, 2013).

DISTRIBUTION AND COURSE

Psychological disorder, for example, ODD are considered as the most widely recognized youth mental sicknesses that require mental execution (Olfson et al., 2014). In spite of the fact that there is commonly a high pattern, the commonness of ODD announced in clinical examinations fluctuates extraordinarily (1% - 11%). Network test information shows that the commonness in certain populaces can be as high as 15.6% (Munkvold et al., 2011). Outpatient thinks about have announced a high extent of clinical indications of ODD, in light of the fact that the referral rate is somewhere in the range of 28% and 65% (Boylan et al., 2007). There are likewise noteworthy contrasts in ARI introductions dependent on age, sex, and ecological variables.

However, ODD manifestations generally show up in the preschool years and once in a while look more slow than in immaturity. Despite the fact that specialists accept that kids' personality influences ODD, there are no particular organic or hereditary expectations for this issue (Loeber et al., 2009). Albeit ODD manifestations regularly show up prior, the nature and seriousness of these indications frequently change during pubescence and early adulthood. Truth be told, there is an unmistakable connection between the improvement of ODD and two social issue (CD) and despondency (Burke et al., 2010; Rowe et al., 2010).

Sex explicit contrasts announced in ODD show that young men meet the criteria more regularly than young ladies

(1.4: 1 in pre and grade school years; APA, 2013). Be that as it may, sexual orientation explicit contrasts have all the earmarks of being distinctive in puberty and past (Munkvold et al., 2011). While young ladies have an expanded danger of encountering melancholy after ODD (Burke et al., 2010), young men are bound to create CD (Rowe et al., 2010).

Ecological elements that are known to add to the episode of activities incorporate expanded family strife and worry for guardians, just as a few financial factors (Cunningham and Boyle, 2002; Lavigne et al., 2012). The information accessible so far show that ODD side effects are most straightforwardly revealed by family reports about parental pressure and in general poor family working (Lavigne et al., 2012). The connection between these logical elements and the improvement of ODD emerges from Gerald Patterson's (1982) depiction of "constrained family forms". what's more, conflicting child rearing.

The advancement of ODD side effects frequently shows a consistent increment in seriousness after some time, which regularly proceeds until the determination of CD, melancholy or different genuine emotional well-being issues. Simultaneous ailments with different ailments frequently convolute the improvement of ODD. Indeed, this is by all accounts a standard as opposed to a special case, in light of the fact that practically half of every ODD case have ADHD simultaneously (Martel et al., 2012; Willcutt et al., 2012) and 40% report critical uneasiness side effects (Drabick et al. ., 2010; Greene et al., 2002) and 12% were determined to have sadness (Stoep et al., 2012).

On the off chance of a downturn, at that point pursues the beginning of youth ODD, the most ideal approach to anticipate this is from the rise of the negative impacts of ODD. Moreover, youngsters who have progressively prevailing side effect difficulties and hostile practices regularly change from ODD to later manifestations that are increasingly illustrative of CD. There is an expected connection of 0.81 among ODD and Cd side effects, which at last mirrors a significant level of side effect comorbidity (Boden et al., 2010; Loeber et al., 2009). Notwithstanding solid proof that ODD backings the expectation of social and enthusiastic issues later on, it is as yet hazy whether its job is causal, prodromal, or only an indication of future issues (Burke and Loeber, 2010).

At last, it is essential to recognize the essential manifestations and the formative adventure of ODD and the side effects of recently presented DMDD. By and large, more profound and tireless negative states of mind and progressively visit and extreme episodes are more quality of DMDD than ODD (APA, 2013). In any case, Leibenluft (2011) shows that 84.9% of youngsters with DMDD additionally meet DSM criteria for long lasting learning. Treatment is imperative to recognize these two conditions with respect to treatment choices, on the grounds that psychosocial intercessions are typically favored in ODD, while in DMDD psychopharmacological mediations may must be considered.

PHARMACOLOGICAL TREATMENT

Pharmacological examinations managing the treatment of ODD are restricted. This intercession is hard to consider in light of the fact that the hidden side effects are frequently connected with Disc (Loeber et al., 2009). Consequently, numerous pharmacological examinations look at ODD/CD manifestations from animosity and passionate dysregulation, disturbing a person's finding instead of concentrating on explicit, incapacitating side effects. The second explanation behind the absence of writing is the high comorbidity of ODD in different sicknesses, for example, ADHD or nervousness and temperament issue. Albeit numerous medications used to treat this comorbid condition can likewise help mitigate the outer manifestations of medical procedure, the proof and organic instruments for improving resistance conduct stay hazy.

With just a couple of studies concentrating on Circle pharmacological treatment and there is solid proof of psychosocial intercessions, clinical practice parameters built up by the American Institute of Kid and Juvenile Psychiatry (AACAP) express that "Medication young people with OD are explicitly viewed as accommodating, palliative and unreasonable" and " ought not be the main mediation in the working room "(Steiner et al., 2007, p. 137). Moreover, a universal accord explanation on ODD prescribes that pharmacological administration of ODD without cautious mental comorbidities is restricted to patients who:

(1) Don't profit by psychosocial intercessions or

(2) Demonstrate the degree of animosity or conduct of extraordinary issue (Kutcher et al., 2004; Steiner et al., 2007).

Explicit pharmacological viability reads for kids with ODD have inspected Divalproex sodium (Depakote), lithium salt (Lithobid) or atypical antipsychotics, for example, risperidone (Risperdal). A randomized clinical preliminary and two open name thinks about with divalproex sodium (DVPX) indicated a critical decrease in "threatening vibe" in moderately aged kids with ODD (Donovan et al., 1997, 2000; Saxena et al., 2010). Lithium salt has been utilized widely for the treatment of hostility for a long time. Be that as it may, they are basically proposed for episodes of pediatric bipolar disorder. Just a couple of controlled examinations exploring the adequacy of lithium salts in conduct and hostility issues in youngsters and youths (Campbell et al., 1995; Malone et al., 2000; Rifkin et al., 1997), none were explicit for ODD. Atypical antipsychotics have gotten more prominent observational help for the treatment of ODD, particularly for forceful side effects. Risperidone is the most often concentrated of these atypical (Papadopoulos et al., 2006), albeit most research on unadulterated PRA (i.e. without comorbidities) is constrained to youngsters with normal knowledge (Aman et al., 2002); Snyder et al., 2002). While these examinations give some help to conduct improvement, they additionally report huge disorder (e.g., low intelligence level, brief span of treatment, flawed follow-up stage, utilization of a mix of medications) and significant levels of reactions (98%; Safe et al., 2002; Snyder et al., 2002).

About portion of kids determined to have ODD experience the ill effects of ADHD comorbidity (Kutcher et al., 2004). Psychostimulant, which is considered as the principle treatment for ADHD, likewise offers potential advantages for the treatment of side effects of externalizing comorbid ODD (Swanson et al., 2001). Methylphenidate is generally excellent in both open mark considers (e.g. Serra-Pinheiro et al., 2004) and in controlled examinations (e.g. Kolko et al., 1999; Pliszka et al., 2000) to decrease psychological disorder and hostility notwithstanding improving manifestations The hidden ADHD. Ongoing examinations have additionally indicated that atomoxetine, a specific inhibitor of norepinephrine reuptake (NRI), is powerful against ODD side effects when utilized with ADHD (Blasts et al., 2008; Dell'Agnello et al.). , 2009; Dittmann et al., 2011).

The fundamental preferred position of atomoxetine treatment over incitement treatment is the more extended length of the impact, which can beat the manifestations that show up in the first part of the day and night when the stimulatory impacts normally die down. After methylphenidate and atomoxetine, algo-2-adrenergic receptor agonists, for example, clonidine and guanfacin can be viewed as second-line drugs for the treatment of side effects of ODD and ADHD comorbidity. Clinical examinations with clonidine or guanfacin alone or in blend with incitement treatment have been appeared to lessen restriction in youngsters with ADHD co-morbidities (e.g. Connor et al., 2010; Palumbo et al., 2008); Be that as it may, on account of the potential for genuine overdoses, there is impressive alert (Hazell, 2010). Current worldwide treatment rules bolster the clinical utilization of alpha-2 agonists in kids with ADHD and Disc co-morbidities, extreme ODD or tic issue, and in youngsters with ADHD and ODD comorbidities that don't react decidedly to energizers. or on the other hand from atomoxetine. (Turgay, 2009).

To a lesser degree, pharmacological medications for tasks with AMD comorbidities have been considered. Two ongoing examinations have indicated promising help for specific serotonin reuptake inhibitor (SSRI) treatment in teenagers with Sphere and comorbid issue and state of mind issue (Jacobs et al., 2010; Kodish et al., 2011). In any case, the present parameters of AACAP clinical practice for

ODD show that there is right now insufficient proof to help the utilization of SSRIs to treat ODD indications (Steiner et al., 2007). With the presentation of the new DMDD analytic classification, which is currently used to outline sort of issue, SSRI guidelines focus on the DMDD populace instead of a subset of youngsters with comorbid ODD and AMD (Leibenluft, 2011).

ADVANTAGE OF PHARMACOLOGICAL TREATMENT OF ODD

Pharmacological medicines ought not be considered as first-line mediations in ODD, however as auxiliary treatment choices that are possibly offered after proof based psychosocial intercessions or when comorbid conditions require adjustment. In spite of the fact that reviews have taken a gander at the impacts of a few medications used to treat Circle, just a couple have considered ODD without comorbidity. Past information show that risperidone offers the most potential advantages for forceful hostility, yet scarcely any advantages for expanding indications of rebelliousness or other social issues. Risperidone considers are constrained to youngsters with scholarly handicaps, and regular negative symptoms, for example, laziness, extrapyramidal impacts, and weight gain show that extraordinary alert is required.

Related to ADHD, the most grounded observational proof recommends the utilization of a mix of energizers and atomoxetine to treat ODD. Methylphenidate is most ordinarily utilized for use with the potential for noteworthy advantages from ADHD-related infringement and responsive hostility. Atomoxetine must be constrained to what is viewed as a negligible incitement response or has symptoms. At present, alpha-2 agonists, for example, clonidine and guanfacin have minimal help for the treatment of ADHD and ODD comorbidities. Joined with uneasiness and temperament issues, pharmacological information for the treatment of ODD show the advantages of utilizing SSRIs that bode well.

PSYCHOLOGICAL TREATMENT

Proof based psychosocial intercessions are prescribed as the best quality level for the consideration of youngsters with ORD. The mediations in this area are bolstered by Randomized Controlled Treatments (RCTs) that have been done well and have been found to surpass the control conditions without treatment or holding up records. In this manner, these psychosocial medications are characterized as liable to be compelling or decided dependent on criteria initially set by the APA working gathering on exactly bolstered treatment (Chamberlain and Hollon, 1998). Notwithstanding demonstrating stable positive treatment results, these projects show longitudinal and by and large impacts, both successful and perpetual mediations (McNeil et al., 1991). Child development projects, particularly for more youthful youngsters, are one of the most ordinarily read treatments for kids with conduct issues, for example, ODD and are suggested as a first-line approach (Eyberg et al., 2008). Intercessions for youths in youth and puberty for the most part center around individual or gathering sessions with kids. Kids in this formative stage have a more noteworthy capacity to utilize a psychological social methodology wherein they are the primary on-screen characters in change. Be that as it may, given that parental contradiction conduct, family struggle, and family precariousness are identified with the improvement and upkeep of psychological disorder in kids (Frick et al., 1992; Patterson, 1982), youngster well disposed mediations regularly incorporate parts of care. The following is a review of controlled proof based mediations that have gotten the best research support for the treatment of ODD, just as extra projects that accentuate a similar proof based standards.

PARENT-TRAINING SYSTEM

Parent-Children Interaction therapy (PCIT) is a conduct program to teach guardians about youngsters matured 2 to 7 years (McNeil and Hembree-Kigin, 2010). The run of the mill structure of PCIT comprises of an hour long week by week treatment session in which the advisor, as a rule behind a single direction reflect, trains guardians in managing their kid's capacities. PCIT comprises of two stages: Children coordinated Communication (CDI) and Parent-Direct Interaction (PDI). CDI sessions center around cultivating positive investment and effectively overlooking aptitudes. Methods for characterizing limits and order are featured during the PDI to help guardians reliably and typically seek after conduct systems. Guardians figure out how to accommodate their glow and responsiveness with requests and order. PCIT advisors code parent-youngster collaborations to quantify the advancement of child rearing abilities and decide their dominance of aptitudes. PCIT fulfillment relies upon acing the particular capacities of guardians, on their faith in autonomous treatment of their youngsters' conduct and on their evaluation of Eyberg's stock (ECBI) for kids' conduct in ordinary regions (Eyberg) and Pincus, 1999).

Helping the Noncompliant Child (HNC) is a program made only for youngsters between the ages 3 and 8 years

(McMahon and Forehand, 2003). Guardians and youngsters are seen together during 60-hour and a half sessions, which happen more than once per week for around 10 weeks. HNC aptitudes are accomplished through remedial demonstrating, pretending among guardians and advisors and through preparing with youngsters in the center and at home. Specialists are prepared in a treatment focus or behind single direction mirrors. Like PCIT, the HNC program comprises of two support stages. In the main stage (separated consideration) guardians learn abilities to improve kids' prosocial conduct (through positive verbal and physical consideration) and to diminish pointless unfortunate conduct (through uplifting feedback and disregard systems). The subsequent stage (consistence preparing) centers around teaching guardians, giving clear directions and managing viable outcomes (e.g. pausing or losing consent) for rebelliousness with guidelines.

The Incredible Years (IY) learning arrangement comprises of three preparing programs: kids' projects (IY-CT, ages 3 to 8), parent programs (IY-PT, ages 2 to 10) and instructor programs for kids as long as 12 years (Webster Stratton and Reid, 2003). Each IY program is conveyed via prepared mediators and executed in a gathering design. Parent and youngster programs are normally offered for 12 to 22 weeks alongside 2 to 3 hour sessions. Sessions incorporate video outlines customized to explicit objective gatherings (e.g. guardians, educators, or gatherings of kids). Representations incorporate testing circumstances that frequently happen, trailed by bunch dialogs contrasting wasteful and powerful ways with manage issue circumstances.

Triple P - Positive Child Development Project is a treatment created for youngsters from birth to 12 years old, with expansions for a very long time 13 to 16 years, and with the point of reinforcing the certainty and capacities of guardians (Sanders, 1999). Triple P can be sent separately, in gatherings, controlled alone or in a blend of these arrangements. Triple P is staggered (levels 1 to 5), and families take an interest in specific levels relying upon the seriousness of the youngsters' conduct issues. Level 4 (Standard Triple P) and Level 5 (Improved Triple P) get the most exact help (Eyberg et al., 2008). Triple P Standard incorporates ten child rearing sessions for people or eight gatherings on themes, for example, extraordinary consideration, successful requests, intelligent results, rest and pausing. Level 5 is an all-encompassing variant that incorporates home visits and three to five extra sessions identified with family pressure factors (for instance, parental melancholy, conjugal clash; Sanders et al., 2003).

Parent Management Training-Oregon Model (PMTO) is bolstered for use with the broadest age gathering of kids (3 to 12 years; Patterson et al., 1975). PMTO can be accessible in gathering or single configuration. Singular family gatherings most recent an hour and are held each week for around 25-30 weeks. Gathering sessions most recent an hour and a half and most recent 14 weeks per week. Treatment likewise incorporates midweek advisors to advance effective home mediations and aptitudes gathering. Advisors instruct guardians through pretending and capacity displaying in five regions: advancing aptitudes (e.g. impetus frameworks and prizes for positive conduct), defining limits, checking, critical thinking and positive investment. The request for content substance and the time dispensed for every ability differs relying upon the necessities of the family and the degree of support of the kid in the session. Acing child rearing aptitudes is an essential for learning disciplinary methodologies, for example, B. viable direction and predictable and quiet utilization of results (e.g. pausing, nullification of privileges) of infringement.

INTERVENTIONS FOR CHILDREN DEVELOPMENT

Critical thinking aptitudes preparing utilizes intellectual rebuilding and critical thinking abilities (e.g., issue recognizable proof, basic leadership, basic leadership, and viewpoint) to enable ODD youth to defeat relational troubles (Kazdin, 2010). This treatment is expected for kids somewhere in the range of 7 and 13 years and comprises of 12 weeks of individual treatment sessions with a length of 30 to 50 minutes. The advisor utilizes intuitive activities, games, demonstrating and pretending in different situations that are frequently experienced by kids and uses financially savvy tokens with reaction costs. The main session centers around youngsters' contribution, yet guardians are all the more effectively engaged with ensuing sessions to rehearse day by day situations that challenge and assist kids with condensing their abilities in utilizing the home (Kazdin, 2010).

Anger Control Training (ACT) is a gathering based gathering intercession that objectives negative, testing, and unfriendly conduct towards school specialists (Larson and Lochman, 2002). Eighteen (60-an hour and a half) week by week sessions for kids matured 8-12 years managing intellectual adapting techniques, familiarity with physiological methodologies, points of view and critical thinking aptitudes. After the aptitudes improvement session, members watch recordings of other youngsters experiencing relational troubles and afterward talk about option suitable social reactions. Kids take an interest in job tests to pick elective aptitudes utilizing procedures that have been presented in the program. Shutting sessions offer kids the chance to act in genuine circumstances and apply new abilities as opposed to responding with difficulties or hostility. Similarly, adapting power is a clinical program created as an augmentation of ACT. Adapting Force offers balanced learning costs for kids and conduct segments for childcare (Lochman et al., 2010).

In spite of the fact that the above projects have been most experimentally bolstered, there are additionally numerous mediations that depend entirely on proof based rules that characterize these projects - for instance, Barkleys Rebellious Kids (2013), Kapalka (2007) Child rearing Your Out-of-Children Control , Casdin and Rotella (2009) Casdin's Technique for Bringing up Testing and Green Children (2010) The Dangerous Youngster. Each program underscores the utilization of uplifting feedback to advance suitable conduct, increment group viability, distinguish steady snags, and apply non-physical/non-disciplinary control methods. Each program likewise includes methodologies that can be the focal point of family care. For instance, the 10-session program by Barkley (10) Barkley (2013) offers proactive and responsive procedures to manage negative practices, (for example, crisis the board, break, issue forecast and school coordinated effort). PMT by Kazdin and Rotella (2009) joins the arrangement of conduct into sessions and instructs guardians to clarify meanings of social objectives and to reinforce a steady way to deal with the ideal outcomes. Notwithstanding managing contentious and testing conduct, Kapalka (2007) underscores procedures for managing enthusiastic dysregulation and conduct wild, particularly for circumstances of regular issues, for example, changes between exercises, during schoolwork and during work. You are in broad daylight. In like manner, Greene's (2010) Unstable Kid program features the troubles in controlling feelings and psychological adaptability in youngsters who become touchy. Green shows guardians how to perceive interruption notice signs, how to take out parental conduct that can cause disturbance, and how to "bit by bit change" it with the goal that youngsters can think about decisions when baffled.

ADVANTAGES OF PSYCHOTHERAPY FOR ODD TREATMENT

Early intercessions with psychosocial mediations are demonstrated in ODD to be modest as well as powerful as clinical practice. Positive treatment results for these RCT mediations have been shown which give a solid proof base to their utilization in the treatment of ODD (e.g. Webster-Stratton et al., 2004). In ensuing investigations, this intercession additionally indicated that treatment was kept up for a long time after treatment finished (e.g. Forgatch et al., 2009). Given the proceeded with positive restorative impacts after treatment, psychosocial intercessions are the highest quality level for youngsters with ORD and are an appealing decision for families, networks and specialists who recommend essential consideration (Edidin et al., 2012).

Psychosocial intercessions in ODD spotlight on youngsters' learning and authority methods that make new models of solid communications and negative obligatory cycle issue and lead to testing conduct (Patterson, 1982). Abilities learned in care would then be able to be utilized when treatment is finished, with follow-up care done varying. In correlation, keeping up a psychotropic medicine plan requires cautious checking and consistent support during drug use. Also, medicates obviously don't demonstrate the capacity to change examples of collaboration between kids or parental figures and are along these lines not a reasonable long haul arrangement. Moreover, meds for youngsters with psychological disorder offer a wide range of results relying upon their age and comorbidity.

COMBINED TREATMENT

There is an absence of research identified with psychosocial and pharmacological intercessions in the treatment of Circle. This is generally because of the way that psychosocial approaches are favored as mediations, while drugs are regularly utilized as a guide in the treatment of comorbidities or to battle hostility (Steiner et al., 2007; Turgay, 2009). In spite of the absence of research on pharmacotherapy for ODD, clinical practice parameters built up by AACAP (Steiner et al., 2007) keep on indicating that effective ODD treatment frequently requires multimodal treatment. What's more, the AACAP prescribes that specialists create singular consideration plans for kids and young people, since singular treatment modalities can shift from patient to understanding (Steiner et al., 2007).

At present, existing information on joined treatment of ODD must be extrapolated from examines that emphasis fundamentally on different issue of psychological disorder, to be specific ADHD (MTA Agreeable Gathering, 1999; Swanson et al., 2001). MTA thinks about look at the viability of different medicines for ADHD (MTA Helpful

Gathering, 1999). A subset of tests from this examination demonstrated comorbid OR3, and auxiliary investigation indicated that medications joined with social treatment were altogether more successful than treatment alone, despite the fact that the impact was little (Swanson et al., 2001). Swanson et al. included that, from the outset, the low effect of psychosocial intercessions may be mostly because of the inconstancy of dependability and adequacy of treatment between areas. A few sites discover moderate to huge beneficial outcomes for psychosocial care, while others discover little to huge negative impacts (p. 177). Further mix ponders utilizing standard social treatment are expected to show extra clinical advantages of the impacts of the medication in kids with ADHD and ODD comorbidities (just as in kids with "unadulterated" ODD).

ADVANTAGE OF COMBINED TREATMENT FOR ODD

There is no ongoing exploration managing the utilization of a mix of pharmacological and psychosocial medications for ODD populaces alone. This may be a valid justification on the grounds that viable conduct treatment is accessible for ODD. In light of the absence of proof to help pharmacological intercessions and solid proof for parental mediations and mediations to manufacture youngster related abilities (see Edidin et al., 2012, for survey), psychosocial intercessions are unmistakably the best treatment for ODD. Since just a couple of pharmacological investigations have attempted to treat ODD explicitly, further examinations are expected to evaluate the viability of adding pharmacological help to first-line psychosocial mediations.

Current practice parameters can show that energizers,

alpha-2 agonists, or even atypical antipsychotics are added to psychosocial treatment to treat kids' conduct that is fundamentally forceful, problematic, or inert to confirm based treatment. Be that as it may, these rules depend on the agreement of clinical specialists, not on observational information from RCTs or even open examinations. Hence, pharmacological consideration must be painstakingly viewed as while treating "unadulterated" PSA indications, considering unanswered inquiries concerning their long haul adequacy and wellbeing in this populace. Unfavorable medication related occasions, (for example, weakness, sickness, tics, weight addition and conceivable overdose) can exceed the advantages for some youngsters. Along these lines, specialists should cautiously examine this issue with their families. From a pragmatic perspective, the requirement for tranquilize titration can likewise present huge difficulties because of the absence of distributed research or medication calculations for this populace. At long last, the utilization of ODD medications is viewed as boundless, in light of the fact that the US Nourishment and Medication Organization just gives assent for comorbid sicknesses, for example, ADHD. This is another explanation behind alert (Charach et al., 2011). .

Before directing RCT treatment methodologies for kids with ODD, further research is expected to break down the impacts of different psychotropic medications on explicit ODD indications, which are segregated or analyzed with measurable control on the impacts of comorbid manifestations (e.g. ADHD). After this field of study has been stretched out to ISPA itself or as an essential objective of treatment, scientists can break down the general adequacy of different medications in blend with the psychosocial intercessions of decision referenced somewhere else in this part.

Restriction challenge issue is a condition with a high base level that causes noteworthy conduct, enthusiastic, and relational troubles for the analyzed individual and family, instructor, and companions. Without treatment, ORD side effects will in general persevere and intensify after some time (Shaw et al., 2005). They frequently progress from psychological disorder in youth to puberty and adulthood and are portrayed by enthusiastic issues or hostile to social practices, for example, wrongdoing and viciousness. Luckily, kids and young people with ODD have been appeared to react emphatically to intercessions both during treatment and in long haul follow-up thinks about. It is all the more promising that psychosocial medicines are best for over the top enthusiastic issue, which is the reason pharmacotherapy isn't required. Actually, investigations of pharmacological intercessions so far are so little and hazy that treatment isn't suggested as a possibility for blend ODD treatment except if the hazard or side effects of comorbidity show that extra help is required (Steiner et al., 2007). There are numerous social treatments for introductory treatment comprising of parental preparing or kid related psychotherapy in individual and gathering groups.

The impossible drive elements that go past the person's capacity to control them are the hypothetical starting points of psychological disorder. As talked about in past sections, absence of poise can be brought about by organic variables, (for example, diminished serotonin levels, as detailed by Worbe et al., 2014), formative occasions, (for example, youngster misuse, as examined by Brodsky) and Stanley, 2008) or a mix of both. Poor discretion can cause rash conduct. Such individuals regularly can't foresee negative outcomes for their conduct and don't adequately defer satisfaction (Barkley, 1997). Harmed restraint can likewise cause deficiencies in enthusiastic guideline, a center component of most state of mind and personality disorder. Passionate guideline, combined with lack of caution, is a significant conduct part that contradicts social standards, (for example, reserved personality disorder) and causes critical issue (particularly state of mind and personality disorder).

Hasty individuals will in general experience expanded movement/engine excitement, give less consideration to their condition and not prepare. Crash (2013) contends that absence of restraint and animosity is regular among indiscreet individuals. This characterizes animosity as conduct that must mischief or harm other living things. As talked about beneath, hostility is frequently a significant helpful objective in the Major Depressive Disorder (MDD), bipolar disorder (BD), Borderline Personality Disorder (BPD) and Antisocial Personality Disorder (ASPD).

Upsetting rash driving forces are related with progressively forceful and rough conduct, more infringement of the law, higher backslide rates and higher suicide rates that are attempted and done. As indicated by Moeller et al. (2001), impulsivity is increasingly regular in individuals with temperament and personality disorder than other mental patients or solid controls, which is the reason this symptomatic class is so significant in the treatment of psychological disorder. Moeller et al. (2001) included that every treatment for disposition and personality disorder should explicitly concentrate on rash treatment to limit manifestations and reaction to treatment.

MOOD DISORDER AS A DISRUPTIVE PSYCHOLOGICAL DISORDER

Suicide is the most pulverizing and preventable psychological disorder, and misery is the most well-known issue of suicide conduct (Communities for Infection Control and Counteractive action, National Place for Damage Anticipation and Control, 2012). Suicide is one of the main sources of death and significant general medical issues all through the world. Impulsivity and hostility are increasingly basic among discouraged individuals who attempt to end it all (Corruble et al., 2003; Oquendo et al., 2004) than the individuals who don't. In their 2005 investigation of men who ended it all, Dumais et al. (2005) found that more youthful suicide unfortunate casualties (18-40 years) were more indiscreet and forceful than non-self-destructive discouraged controls of a similar age or more established suicide exploited people. More youthful suicide exploited people additionally utilize harder approaches to slaughter their lives than more seasoned unfortunate casualties. Despite the fact that the creators don't give hypotheses about the motivations to this revelation, natural contrasts, (for example, higher testosterone levels and immature prefrontal cortex that controls drive control) among more youthful and more established subjects appear to bode well. The creators likewise report that the danger of suicide in discouraged individuals increments with forceful/hasty personality disorder and liquor misuse/compulsion.

Corruble et al. (2003) analyzed the effect of impulsivity on suicide rates. They recognized three hasty measurements: loss of conduct control, arranged impulsivity and intellectual. The creators found a positive relationship between ongoing suicidal endeavors and expanded loss of control and psychological impulsivity.

Swann and others (2005) found that imprudence in bipolar subjects added to the danger of self-destructive conduct and that subjects with the most deadly suicide endeavors had the most noteworthy hasty qualities. In an ensuing report, Swann et al. (2009a) found that impulsivity as a trademark happens more as often as possible in bipolar subjects than non-bipolar ones. In like manner, Swann et al. (2009b) found that rash seriousness was emphatically identified with the beginning of indications, increasingly visit hyper scenes or discouragement, and more suicide endeavors. Impulsivity incorporates consideration issue and response hindrances, and individuals with bipolar disorder are influenced in the two viewpoints, which makes postponing endowments progressively troublesome and prompts increasingly damaging activities. What's more, the seriousness of the infection is legitimately corresponded with the pace of decrease in response restraint.

ANALYTICAL CONDITIONS

Extreme burdensome issue in the US is a significant reason for inability, diminished profitability, and social insurance costs (Greenberg et al., 2003). Individuals with this issue are described by misery/despondency for the majority of the day and anhedonia for at any rate two weeks. They have critical brokenness in significant aspects of their lives, for example, B. social cooperation, proficient portrayal or self-care. The nearness of extra touchiness and impulsivity is adversely identified with forecast. This is the most comorbid with tension issue, as found in the 2005 National Overview on Infection (Kessler et al., 2005). Critical relationships were: summed up tension issue or Stray (r = 0.62), agoraphobia (r = 0.52) and post-horrendous pressure issue (r = 0.50). Liquor fixation was noteworthy at r = 0.37 and chronic drug use at r = 0.40.

Bipolar disorder is the most serious emotional episodes disorder. Individuals with this determination experience outrageous emotional episodes among misery and insanity, in some cases both simultaneously. Craziness is related with decreased requirement for rest, high vitality levels, sentiment of size, directed conduct is too high or more all hazardous hasty conduct, (for example, wantonness, betting, tranquilize misuse or self animosity) of others). Scenes of despondency in BD are like serious gloom. Individuals can likewise have a blended mind-set express (a mix of extreme discouragement and hyper highlights) which is conceivably progressively perilous on the grounds that an expansion in psychomotor vitality can cause hasty/fierce activities. Like MDD, BD is the most comorbid for uneasiness. The most elevated connections for this issue were: agoraphobia (r = 0.52), alarm issue (r = 0.51) and Stray (r = 0.49).

The fifth version of the Diagnostic and Statistical Guide to Mental Disorders (DSM-5) incorporates another analysis of mind-set issue (DMDD) for kids with serious crabbiness and hyperarosis, like madness and hypomania, however not plainly characterized. have hyper and burdensome scenes that are normal for bipolar disorder. The finding was made to a limited extent to conquer the debate encompassing the sensational increment in the quantity of youngsters with bipolar disorder in the previous 15 years and the typical treatment of these kids with state of mind stabilizers, a large number of which have huge potential for risky symptoms. In a writing audit, Leibenluft (2011) contends that infrequent fractiousness in kids is a phenotype that is not the same as the more great bipolar disorder saw in kids with clear disposition stages. In the longitudinal investigation he inspected, non-infrequent fractiousness in kids was moderately normal and was decidedly identified with an expanded danger of creating bipolar nervousness and despondency in adulthood, however not bipolar disorder. He additionally found that the degree of family bipolar disorder expanded altogether in kids with exemplary bipolar side effects, however was not higher than the overall public in youngsters with abnormal crabbiness. Leibenluft (2011) characterizes serious state of mind issue as touchiness with outrageous and tenacious displeasure related with misery, and reports that debilitated youngsters experience the ill effects of these indications (essentially DMDD, as characterized in DSM-5). genuine manifestations like bipolar disorder.

DISTRIBUTION AND COURSE

In light of replication information from the 2005 National Comorbidity Study (Kessler et al., 2005), lifetime MDD commonness is 16.6% of the grown-up populace, however DSM-5 reports lower pervasiveness following a year from 7% (American) Mental Affiliation [APA], 2013). These distinctions may be because of the age section of the investigation - the commonness of MDD in the 18-29 age bunch is multiple times more noteworthy than in the 60+ age gathering (APA, 2013). Untreated burdensome scenes can last from 6 to year and a half, however overall around 8 months. Scenes treated normally last from about a month and a half to a quarter of a year. In sorrow treated with prescription, scenes normally return, particularly if antidepressants are halted rashly. The normal age at pattern is 14.5 years.

Manifestations of bipolar disorder as a rule happen late in youthfulness, yet can happen whenever from early adolescence to the 50's. As per an examination by Brotman et al. (2006) the lifetime predominance for bipolar disorder (N = 1,420) is 0.1%, and DSM-5 allows a year pervasiveness of 0.6% (APA, 2013). In few individuals determined to have bipolar disorder, treatment builds side effects to the point that treatment is never again required, however this is progressively commonplace of hyper scenes and gloom. The likelihood of a second hyper scene is practically 100% (Kessler et al., 2005), yet with treatment the hazard drops to half. A high rate (82.9%) of bipolar patients are named genuine and frequently require inpatient care. At any rate half of cases start before the age of 25. Individuals with bipolar disorder have higher capture and confinement rates for individuals without psychological sickness and are over-spoken to in penitentiaries and jails. You have more work interferences and relational clashes.

DMDD circulation and advancement data isn't yet

accessible in light of the fact that this is another occurrence that was first enlisted at DSM-5. Brotman et al. (2006) recently detailed a lifetime commonness of indications, for example, DMDD (N = 1,420) of 3.3%. The DSM-5 gauges the commonness somewhere in the range of 6 and a year in the scope of 2% to 5% and shows that the manifestations of this issue will in general decline in adulthood (APA, 2013).

PERSONALITY DISORDER AS A PSYCHOLOGICAL DISORDER

Impulsivity, forcefulness and aggressiveness, which are basic in personality disorder, are viewed as steady highlights that are more impervious to remedial mediations than manifestations in different issue (Moeller et al., 2001). For individuals to meet the criteria for personality disorder, they should have "changeless examples" of internal experience and conduct that are essentially affected by their way of life, and they should have scatters in any event two of the accompanying four territories: contorted information, passionate unsettling influences, drive control impeded and poor relational capacity. These qualities must exist paying little mind to individuals' mind-sets. BPD and ASPD are the two personality disorder regularly connected with psychological disorder and the main personality disorder in which psychological disorder are recorded as the primary indications (APA, 2013).

Lawrence et al. (2010) intently analyze the job of impulsivity in BPD and separation impulsivity into two classifications: inclination for quick fulfillment and dismissal of long haul rewards. They found that individuals with BPD will in general promptly fulfill and dismiss long haul blessings paying little heed to negative feelings and sentiments of dismissal. The creators infer that the impulsivity innate in BPD is trademark and not reactionary. This discovering is significant for treatment arranging and forecast.

The distinction among rash and non-incautious conduct is generally apparent in ASPD. In their investigation, Moeller et al. (2001) partition detainees by ASPD into two classifications: the individuals who submit rash animosity and the individuals who purposefully submit hostility. They found solid organic markers on incautious subjects, yet not on the individuals who arranged their violations. In particular, hasty occupants have lower verbal capacities and lower top P300 amplitudes actuated by potential. Likewise, antiepileptic tranquilizes definitely lessen the forceful conduct of indiscreet detainees, while the forceful conduct of unregistered members isn't diminished. In like manner, Coccarro et al. (1989) found a reduction in 5HT levels in individuals with mind-set and personality disorder who have self-destructive and imprudent/forceful conduct. Moeller et al. (2001) contend that ASPD treatment ought to incorporate heartbeat screening and thought of conceivable organically significant substrates.

To explain the rash job in withdrawn conduct, Swann et al. (2010) contrasted the subjects of male passwords and ASPD with men without psychological disorder. Indiscretion comprises of the powerlessness to completely survey the circumstance before the response (imprudence of the quick response) and the failure to defer the response despite the fact that the prize is higher (indiscreet when deferring finance). The creators found that patients with ASPD experienced incautious issue of fast reaction. The heavier the ASPD, the more hasty.

DIAGNOSIS CONSIDERATION

Introverted personality disorder and BPD are assembled in cluster B (known as the "sensational, enthusiastic, clamorous group") of personality disorder and speak to the most noteworthy predominance of psychological disorder among personality disorder (Moeller et al., 2001). The relationship between personality disorder and other mental determinations is higher in bunch B issue than in cluster A or C disorder (Lenzenweger et al., 2007).

Individuals with ASPD are typically not terrified of their conduct, yet some of the time can claim to show regret and compassion on the off chance that it is to their greatest advantage (for instance before a judge) Such individuals regularly seek after their needs while disregarding the privileges of others. They will in general be hasty, touchy, and forceful. Conduct that goes astray socially from this issue must exist at age 15, must be lasting and can't be better clarified by other psychological disorder.

Marginal personality disorder is one of the most ordinarily considered character pathologies, maybe due to the frequently fierce, ruinous, and rash conduct characteristics that are basic with this disorder. Individuals with BPD will in general show solid and flimsy feelings, in this manner upsetting associations with others. They regularly dread being abandoned and respond viciously and significantly when they deliver retribution on others. They will in general observe the world dressed in high contrast and regularly vary from gauges that are too high to even think about underestimating the individuals around them. You have a flimsy feeling of self and experience issues keeping up a steady and stable way of life. Such individuals for the most part harm themselves and rebuff everyone around them.

Linehan (1993) clarifies that, in contrast to serious gloom, individuals with BPD don't at first experience despondency, yet frequently experience a "full of feeling unsteadiness" episode that can last from a few hours to a few days and doesn't meet the criteria for the turmoil. BPD has issues controlling feelings and can have short bitterness, dread, or outrage. They likewise will in general be hasty and defenseless against self-mutilation, mutilation, and endeavored suicide. Linehan (1993) clarifies that numerous individuals with BPD have utilized outrageous conduct to get the ideal approval if their condition doesn't react to less extraordinary conduct.

DISSEMINATION AND COURSE

As indicated by Lenzenweger et al. (2007), the commonness pace of ASPD in grown-ups in the US is 0.6%, and this figure is higher in men than ladies (around 3: 1). In one examination, Alegria et al. (2013) found that ladies with ASPD were bound to report enthusiastic disregard and sexual maltreatment in youth, just as antagonistic occasions identified with childcare. Ladies displayed more grounded solitary conduct than men in their investigation, however were progressively forceful and bad tempered. Ladies likewise report higher mishap rates, more practical inabilities and less social help than their men. Researchers contend that there must be a sexual orientation explicit treatment program as a result of sex explicit contrasts in the starting point and articulation of standoffish conduct. ASPD is across the board among detainees and is portrayed by consistent association in criminal operations, threatening vibe towards others, deceitfulness and mercilessness. The course of the infection will in general be ceaseless and has a negative association with the underlying rate of solitary conduct and medication misuse (Loeber et al., 1993).

Despite the fact that it is for the most part accepted that BPD is progressively normal in ladies, Award et al. (2008) found no factually huge sexual orientation contrasts (by and large recurrence 5.9%, men 5.6% and ladies 6.2%), albeit a higher level of ladies on treatment was recognized. Indians who are more youthful and not wedded (paying little mind to whether they are isolated, separated, or bereaved) and Indians with lower pay and an excess of training. Yovev et al. (2013) found that youth viciousness (particularly sexual maltreatment and disregard) was a significant indicator of MRF. They likewise found a positive connection between the seriousness of misuse and the seriousness of social manifestations. Expected outcomes for individuals with BPD are more positive than recently suspected. Ongoing investigations report that up to 88% of those influenced experience a huge increment after some time (Award et al., 2008).

COMORBID MIND AND PERSONALITY DISORDER

The state of mind and personality disorder examined here are described by animosity and impulsivity, and the synchronous event of this issue improves the probability of side effects. For instance, Soloff et al. (2000) found that comorbid BPD with extreme burdensome scenes expanded the number and seriousness of suicide endeavors and sadness, while hasty animosity expanded the danger of self-destructive conduct. Despite the fact that BPD explicit impulsivity isn't in itself an indicator of more investigations or expanded mortality, the blend of static driving forces with discouragement and related misery builds the seriousness and recurrence of suicide endeavors.

There is a solid connection of psychological disorder that are regular in ASPD and BD, particularly those identified with impulsivity. Barzman et al. (2007) discovered high paces of unlawful conduct in youths who had as of late been determined to have BD (53%), and the underlying flare-up of BD was decidedly connected with underage withdrawn conduct, with an improved probability of wrongdoing.

Consequently, Barzman et al. (2007) contend that there is a higher predominance of detainees with BD than in the all inclusive community. Swann and others (2010) found that hasty conduct, for example, sedate maltreatment and suicide endeavors were bound to happen in individuals with comorbid ASPD and BD than in one or different issue. Swann and others (2010) analyzed the impacts of what they called "imprudent attributes" on the seriousness of the illness in individuals with BD, ASPD, and the two consolidated ailments. They view impulsivity as highlights (stable highlights of an individual's conduct ordinarily observed in ASPD) and highlights (stores of expanded arrival of norepinephrine during hyper scenes). The two can pass together and make each other's weight troublesome. Swann and others Individuals who are related to BD or ASPD alone are more imprudent than non-neurotic controls, and individuals with BD are more rash than individuals with ASPD alone, regardless of whether they have comorbid ASPD or not. They presumed that the blend of BD and ASPD negatively affected forecast because of expanded impulsivity. Strikingly, Swann et al. noticed that rashness isn't identified with the seriousness of wrongdoing for individuals with ASPD. They reasoned that expectation was identified with the earnestness of wrongdoing and all the more explicitly identified with the number-crunching character contained in ASPD.

PSYCHOLOGICAL TREATMENT FOR MIND DISORDER

Psychotherapy is suggested for individuals with discouragement who endure critical psychosocial stress, relational clash, comorbid personality disorder, approach psychotherapy suppliers or lean toward treatment. The APA rules Cognitive Behavioral Therapy (CBT), Interpersonal Psychotherapy (IPT) and psychodynamic treatment as proof based psychosocial mediations for misery (APA, 2010). A considerable lot of these medications explicitly manage psychological disorder and side effects.

For instance, in a randomized controlled preliminary, Darker et al. (2005) have demonstrated that CBT is a viable mediation to avert suicide endeavors in individuals who have attempted it previously. In a moderately brief time (around eight sessions), they figured out how to diminish suicide endeavors by up to half. Psychodynamic treatment is additionally demonstrated without anyone else's input. Maina et al. (2005) found that psychodynamic treatment for reduction of burdensome manifestations was superior to anything fake treatment and had a more enduring impact than upkeep treatment following a half year.

Alavi et al. (2013) found that week after week outpatient CBT diminished self-destructive contemplations and misery among discouraged teenagers who endeavored suicide in the previous three months. They contrasted results and subjects in shortlist control status and found a noteworthy decrease in self-destructive ideation (a reduction of 54% - 77%). This discovering is significant on the grounds that suicide is a main source of death among young people, to some extent because of expanded impulsivity and diminished adapting abilities.

On the opposite side of the age range, Heisel et al. (2014) found that a 16-day IPT course decreased self-destructive musings, contemplations of death, and the seriousness of burdensome indications, just as the apparent importance throughout everyday life, social modification, saw social help, and mental prosperity in geriatric patients. This discovering is significant in light of the fact that guardians in the US end it all at regular intervals and more established white men have the most elevated suicide rates among all populace gatherings. Geriatric patients are additionally at most serious danger of encountering critical symptoms from mental medications. Accordingly, decrease of suicide through psychotherapy is significant for this populace.

Miklowitz (2006) announced that in a survey of his examination he found no proof of the adequacy of the prevalence of one psychotherapy methodology looked at over another in the treatment of state of mind disorder. In a fascinating investigation by Kwan et al. (2010), the creators think about patient inclinations as significant factors in reacting to treatment. They found that inclination for methodology reflected what number of patients were experiencing treatment, including whether they began treatment, stayed in care, went to sessions, and had a positive helpful relationship. These elements at last impact treatment results and decrease burdensome side effects when inclinations are considered. The creators reason that it is essential to think about patient perspectives, information, and assessments about various medicines while picking a restorative methodology, since inability to watch these elements can distance patients and lessen understanding consistence.

So also, Givens et al. (2007) found that ethnicity essentially impacted melancholy care inclinations. In their investigation, African-Americans, Asians, and Latinos favored psychotherapy over misery over pharmacology, in light of the fact that the larger part didn't accept that downturn was organic and upper addictive. Rather, subjects anticipate that exhortation and supplication should be progressively compelling.

Bipolar disorder regularly requires tranquilize treatment, particularly in situations where side effects are progressively serious and psychotherapy is frequently utilized notwithstanding medicine treatment. Be that as it may, some examination on the viability of psychotherapy, particularly on the overwhelming indications of BD, is developing. In a little report by Van Dijk et al. (2013) found, for instance, that CBT was compelling in treating BD and that patients improved their disposition control (which decreased suicide), visited less crisis rooms and included less rationally sick individuals. In another examination by Ives-Deliperi et al. . (2013) found that idea based subjective treatment improves the capacity of patients with bipolar disorder to control their feelings. There is a closeness between care based psychological treatment and CBT, the two of which show patients how to direct their feelings and decrease their impulsivity.

ADVANTAGES OF PSYCHOGICAL TREATMENT FOR MIND DISORDER

Psychotherapy is a learning procedure for defeating indications (counting forceful and rash propensities) and along these lines normally prompts more enduring outcomes than pharmacotherapy. Psychotherapy is foreseen to proceed until the patient picks up the abilities expected to keep up reduction of side effects, accordingly forestalling future scenes. On the other hand, the advantages of the medication generally stop when the patient quits taking it.

Psychotherapy is additionally non-intrusive and doesn't bring associations into the body which can have antagonistic impacts. This is significant when treating kids, geriatric patients, pregnant ladies or patients with comorbidities. In like manner, some mental medications can be deadly whenever taken in high portions. This can be a significant factor in picking mediations for self-destructive patients. For instance, it has been accounted for that the utilization of antidepressants in specific patients, particularly youngsters and youths, at first causes self-destructive contemplations, which is the reason these medications incorporate discovery alerts.

Then again, it as a rule requires some investment for the advantages of psychotherapy to produce results - frequently weeks or months - which probably won't be a possibility for irate patients. Likewise, patients with intense hyper scenes will in general react to treatment and may require prompt pharmacological treatment to guarantee their own security (Forthcoming et al., 2005). Psychotherapy additionally requires additional time and cash, on the grounds that most psychotherapy requires 10-26 week by week or fortnightly sessions of one hour each. On the other hand, the utilization of medications generally requires the primary meeting with the recommending specialist and perhaps a few extra arrangements in the following scarcely any months. For certain individuals, pharmacotherapy is progressively costly and tedious.

PSYCHOLOGICAL TREATMENT OF PEOPLE FROM PERSONALITY DISORDER

As opposed to state of mind disorder, personality disorder are viewed as trademark in nature and will in general be constant and spread, while causing noteworthy relational brokenness and mental trouble. They are considered unquestionably more hard to treat than most different ailments, to some extent in light of the fact that these individuals frequently don't get mental treatment and stop treatment in about 70% of cases (Dingfelder, 2004).

Marginal personality disorder are the most usually concentrated of all personality disorder (maybe on the grounds that the patient's conduct is unstable, dangerous, and regularly hazardous). The most as often as possible read psychotherapy mediation for this issue is CBT created by Marsha Linehan (1987). Since the premise of CBT, a few other restorative strategies that have been exactly approved for the treatment of BPD have risen, including two psychodynamic psychotherapies, move situated psychotherapy (Clarkin and Kemberg, 2004) and mental-based treatments (Bateman and Fonagy, 2009) and others. Psychological social treatment (Circuit Centered Treatment) (Giesen-Bloo et al., 2006).

In an examination by Linehan et al. (2006), the creators contrast the adequacy of CBT and psychotherapy, which isn't subject to conduct in the treatment of self-destructive conduct and the general mental capacity of BPD patients. The creators found that CBT performed superior to differentiate treatment modalities. In particular, the probability that CBT members endeavored suicide was half high (p = 0.005), less hospitalizations were required due to self-destructive musings (p = 0.004), and the probability of halting treatment (p <0.001).) had less mental inpatients (p = 0.007) and less crisis rooms (p = 0.04) than members who got elective consideration.

An examination by Bateman and Fonagy (2009) analyzed mindset based treatment (MBT) with organized clinical administration (SCM) for patients with BPD. The aftereffects of this investigation indicated that the two gatherings had improved results from their staggering side effects, yet members in the MBT bunch demonstrated an increasingly sensational decrease in self-detailed and clinically demonstrated issues, including suicide endeavors and hospitalization. The creators contend that the benefit of this methodology lies in the straightforwardness of the learning procedure, which encourages access to mediations in social insurance and between specialist organizations

CONCLUSION

Poor enthusiastic guideline, combined with elevated levels of imprudent conduct, (for example, suicide endeavors, self-hurting conduct and viciousness against others) is normal among individuals with serious state of mind issue (MDD and BD) and individuals with ASPD and BPD. Impulsivity is significantly increasingly basic when BD is related with personality disorder. The blend of the two pathologies is adversely identified with the seriousness of indications and visualization. There is understanding among ponders looking at that passionate guideline, expanded restraint and rash decrease are fundamental for the effective treatment of mind-set issue and personality disorder referenced previously.

The treatment of this issue must:

(1) Survey the underlying degree of impulsivity and discretion, and

(2) Explicitly improve the conduct of this treatment. In patients who are appropriate for mix treatment, the mix of psychotherapy and pharmacotherapy is by all accounts better than either methodology.

Pharmacotherapy is critical to balance out impulsivity/animosity and quicker states of mind, while psychotherapy assists individuals with understanding their issue and etiology, and successfully treat and treat side effects. Psychotropics help with natural security, while psychotherapy is perpetual and improves long haul work.

In spite of the fact that mix medicines are frequently better, both of these techniques can or can't be utilized simultaneously.